PURR-FECT PLACES TO STAY:
Bed & Breakfasts, Country Inns, and Hotels with Resident Cats

Susan Bard Hall

Letters Etcetera   Chicago, Illinois

PURR-FECT PLACES TO STAY:
Bed & Breakfasts, Country Inns, and Hotels
with Resident Cats

By Susan Bard Hall

Published by:

Letters Etcetera

P.O. Box 811280
Chicago, IL 60681-1280 U.S.A.

We invite bed & breakfasts, country inns, or hotels with resident cats not included in this directory to write to the publisher for possible inclusion in future editions.

Copyright © 1999 by Susan Bard Hall
First printing 1999
Printed in the United States of America

Library of Congress Catalog Card Number: 98-92073
ISBN 0-9666989-0-8

TABLE OF CONTENTS

DEDICATION

This book is dedicated to my family.

To Miriam and Max, my parents, for encouraging me
to be whatever my heart desired and to go wherever
my talents took me.

To Kaye, my sister, for listening and championing
my cause.

To Norman, my husband, for allowing me to visualize,
vocalize and vent.

And to Taj, my step-cat and "best bud," for inspiring
this book and for being a source of strength, inspiration,
and comfort.

ACKNOWLEDGMENTS

Since one of my favorite parts of a feature film is the credit roll, I want to credit these individuals without whose help this production would not have been possible.

Ken Amundson of Amundson/Drabik & Associates, Inc., Chicago, Illinois, for front and back cover illustrations, book design and production.

Don Drabik and Mary Ellen Merchut of Amundson/ Drabik & Associates for their assistance and cooperation.

Tom Klym of Thomas A. Klym & Associates Ltd., Lincolnshire, Illinois, for accounting and financial advice.

Marvin Green and Anne Jentry of Jentry-Green PC, Chicago, Illinois, for legal advice.

Marsha Carter-Waite of Associated Bank, Chicago, Illinois, for banking services.

Mary Foley Billingsley of Historic Hotels of America, Washington, D.C., for leads on hotels with resident cats.

Michael Kardas of Kardas Photography, Chicago, Illinois, for the author photograph.

For front cover photos: Brookside Farm Bed and Breakfast Inn, Dulzura, California; Crystal Dreams Bed & Breakfast, Redstone, Colorado; The Inn at Merridun, Union, South Carolina (photo by Rhonda Gregory, Union, South Carolina); The Painted Lady Bed & Breakfast Inn, Colorado Springs, Colorado (photo by Karen Schulman, Steamboat Springs, Colorado); and The Pembridge Court Hotel, London, England.

For back cover photos: Manchester Highlands Inn, Manchester Center, Vermont (photo by Robert Eichorn, Manchester Center, Vermont); Marshall House Bed & Breakfast Inn, Marshall, North Carolina; and Wild Lane Bed & Breakfast Inn, Loveland, Colorado.

INTRODUCTION

In 1992, my then husband-to-be and I were vacationing at Cheeca Lodge in Islamorada, Florida when I met my first "resident cat" — Cheeca Cat. Petting her, if only for a few minutes, really helped fill the void of leaving my Taj at home.

Two years later, my husband Norman and I spent a few days at The Churchill House Inn in Brandon, Vermont. At the time, Lois and Roy Jackson were the innkeepers and Cinnamon was the resident cat.

Then, while passing through South Haven, Michigan, we stopped to get a brochure at A Country Place Bed and Breakfast and Cottages. Although many b & b's have a no pets policy, I found Lee and Art Niffenegger's explanation quite creative: "Pets not permitted as our friendly resident cat would object." Here was another charming b & b with a resident cat.

I knew if there were three, there were many more. And having observed firsthand the interaction between guests and resident cats, I also knew there were other leisure and business travelers who would prefer to stay at a property where they can pet, talk to, and occasionally cuddle someone else's feline in order to help reduce the withdrawal pangs and fill the void of leaving their own cat companion at home.

Resident cats are a win-win-win for the lodging properties, their guests, and of course, the cats. Bed & breakfasts, country inns, and hotels with resident cats seem cozier and more home-like, which can be a welcome change for travelers who spend several nights away from home and their loved ones.

And these cats, many of which were former strays or shelter cats, receive the attention and affection of property owners and employees, not to mention the often unsolicited, but not unwanted, belly, chin, and head rubs from guests.

Spending time at a property with a resident cat also is a refreshing change of pace for cat fanciers everywhere who, for whatever reason, can't have or don't want their own pet, but would love to spend some quality time with a cat when they're away from home.

For all these traveling cat lovers, this directory is the purr-fect resource to locate b & b's, country inns, and hotels with resident cats in the United States, Canada, and the United Kingdom. **_PURR-FECT PLACES TO STAY:_ Bed & Breakfasts, Country Inns, and Hotels with Resident Cats** is believed to be the first directory to focus exclusively on properties with resident cats.

Every effort has been taken to ensure the accuracy of the information contained in this directory but neither the author nor the publisher assumes responsibility for any omissions or errors, whether typographical or otherwise. When inquiring about availability or making reservations at particular properties, please be sure to verify all information contained here as it is subject to change without notice.

I've had the pleasure of staying at a few of the properties profiled here. But inclusion in this directory does not imply an endorsement of the establishment. Nor does omission signify a lack of endorsement.

If you or someone you know has stayed at a purr-fect place not included in this directory, please use the listing form at the back of the book to pass along the name of the b & b, inn, or hotel for possible inclusion in the next edition.

If you're a cat lover with travel plans in your future, then staying at a quaint bed & breakfast, intimate country inn, or luxury hotel with a resident cat may be just up your alley! When you can't be with the cat you love, stay at a purr-fect place and love the cat you're with!

PREFACE

Many, many thanks to the quaint bed & breakfasts, intimate country inns, and luxury hotels that agreed to be included in what I believe to be the first directory to focus exclusively on properties with resident cats. Without your cooperation and support, this directory could not have come to fruition. I hope that completing my questionnaires was a welcome change of pace from all the thankless but necessary tasks that it takes to ensure a guest's memorable stay. Your responses made me laugh a lot, cry a little, and want to meet each and every one of the 85 cats profiled. I hope my vignettes do the same for your prospective guests.

I also want to thank all the amateur photographers for the wonderful snapshots; I know from experience that cats, as cute and cuddly as they are, are not always the most cooperative of subjects.

It would be a wonderful consequence to this book that other b & b's, country inns, and hotels recognize how much resident cats can add to a guest's stay. Resident cats can help reduce the withdrawal pangs and fill the void of leaving one's own feline companion at home. Resident cats also are a win-win for the properties as well as the cats. B & b's, country inns, and hotels with resident cats seem cozier and more home-like, which can be a welcome change for travelers who spend several nights away from home and their loved ones. And these cats, many of which were former strays or shelter cats, receive the attention and affection of property owners and employees, not to mention the often unsolicited, but not unwanted, belly, chin, and head rubs from guests.

It takes a special breed of innkeeper to have a resident cat. But I cannot stress enough that it must always remain the proprietor's decision to have a resident cat and that should in no way be construed to mean that they are looking to expand their feline family. These establishments are not havens for strays. If you have or know of a cat that needs a caring home, please take them to a place that specializes in placing them with the proper family.

It also takes a special kind of kitty to be a resident cat. And to underscore just how unique each of these cats truly is, of the 85 felines profiled in this directory, the same name appeared only three times. Their names are as individual as they are — their backgrounds, personalities, favorite pastimes, pet sleeping spots, and especially the pawprints they leave on our lives.

But what they all have in common is that their presence makes these b & b's, country inns, and hotels **PURR-FECT PLACES TO STAY.**

HOUSE RULES

The following general rules apply to all listings. Guests should verify specific information as it applies to a particular property when inquiring about availability or making a reservation.

- Because of the resident cat(s), guests' pets are not permitted, unless a particular property indicates otherwise in their individual listing.

- Also, because non-cat lovers and/or those with allergies also frequent these properties, resident cats are not allowed in the guestrooms, unless a particular property indicates otherwise in their individual listing.

- Although these properties have opened their hearts and their homes to needy cats, they should not be considered a haven for strays or unwanted pets. If an individual is seeking a better life for a cat and cannot find a loving home, please take the cat to a place that specializes in placing them with the proper family.

- Because rates are subject to change without notice, please verify them at the time the reservation is made.

- Minimum stays may be required for weekends, holidays, or other special events.

- Rates usually are subject to state, local, and hotel taxes.

- Reservations generally are suggested or required.

- Check with each property for their specific reservation, deposit, and cancellation policies, as well as whether they accept credit cards, travelers checks, or personal checks.

- Check-in/check-out times vary from property-to-property, and special arrangements usually can be accommodated.

NORTHEAST

Massachusetts
West Yarmouth, Cape Cod
— The Manor House Bed & Breakfast, 4-7

New Jersey
Belmar
— The Seaflower - A Bed & Breakfast Inn, 8-10
Cape May
— The Albert Stevens Inn & Cat's Garden, 12-17

Pennsylvania
Bradford
— Glendorn, A Lodge in the Country, 18-21
Jacobus (York)
— Past Purr-fect Bed and Breakfast, 22-23
Newtown
— Hollileif Bed & Breakfast, 24-27

Vermont
Brandon
— The Churchill House Inn, 28-29
— The Lilac Inn, 30-32
Manchester Center
— Manchester Highlands Inn, 34-36

The Manor House
Bed & Breakfast

"The Manor House is a comfortable, relaxing b & b that feels like a home away from home. Let us share our dream with you."

— Liz and Rick Latshaw, Hosts

Whitesocks was a wedding day gift to Liz Latshaw from her husband, Rick. This Tabby was waiting for Liz at their new home immediately after the reception. Liz named her for the adorable black kitten with white paws that she had as a child. Rick, so the story goes, wanted to name her Hairball.

"I disliked the name so much that Rick said if we ever got another cat, we had to name it Hairball," Liz said. "He thought this would deter me from ever getting another cat."

Whitestocks had the Latshaws all to herself until one cold November day when Liz received a telephone call from her mother-in-law that she had discovered a kitten living in their shed.

"I said I would be right over," Liz recalled. "I put Whitesocks in the car and went to meet this kitten. She was so needy we had to have her and Whitesocks agreed. We brought her home and nursed her back to health."

When the Latshaws purchased The Manor House Bed & Breakfast, Whitesocks and **Hairball** became inn cats.

Liz said she was concerned that Hairball, a Calico, wouldn't be comfortable around so many people, but apparently she loves it. She is quite gentle, sometimes shy, and seems to prefer a woman's touch. A word of warning to those who think Hairball wants her belly rubbed when she lies on her back with her paws spread apart.

Whitesocks

during the daytime. She's been known to hide under sink skirts and "attack" guests' feet. She, too, has guestroom privileges and loves to check out their belongings.

"She is often found sleeping in guests' suitcases," Liz said.

One time when Whitesocks was visiting a guest taking a bubble bath, she decided to jump on the edge to get a closer look.

"It was slippery and she ended up falling in," Liz said.

"Some well-meaning guests think this is an invitation to scratch her belly," Liz said. 'They've learned the painful way that she hates it."

She's allowed in the guestrooms, but is more likely to be found in her favorite wicker chair, especially during the winter months. Other favorite pastimes are eating and sleeping, so she's gained a few pounds since the Latshaws adopted her.

"Our skinny little stray is always told by the vet to lose some weight and get some exercise. She would rather not," Liz said. "Rick says you get more movement from a stuffed animal!"

Whitesocks is definitely the more playful of the two. She considers it a game to have the guests open the door *for her* whenever she wants in or out

Hairball

Her curiosity also extends to guests' cars, so when they're ready to leave, Liz or Rick always walks outside if there is any possibility that Whitesocks would inadvertently go home with them.

Just steps from the beach, The Manor House Bed & Breakfast on Cape Cod is a great getaway for those who want to start their day with a leisurely stroll along the bay, watch the sailboats or wind-surfers, whalewatch, read a popular novel from the b & b's reading nook, or simply day-dream.

As Liz and Rick tell their guests, there's no extra charge for the sunshine and the bay breezes, and the beach chairs and tow-els also are complimentary.

As the day progresses, there's sailing, freshwater and saltwa-ter fishing, bicycling, walking/ hiking, tennis, golf, and even horseback riding along the beach at sunset.

During the winter months, cross-country skiing and ice skating are available nearby. Year-round, there's shopping — from antiques to crafts to discount stores — as well as exploring local history.

This Dutch Colonial dates back to the 1920s. Located mid-Cape on the southern side, each of the inn's six guestrooms is named for special little touches of Cape Cod which continue to bring guests back time after time. The Latshaws add their own special touches — fresh cut flowers, candles, and a treat on your pillow — to make each guest's stay even more memo-rable.

The Manor House
Bed & Breakfast

57 Maine Avenue
West Yarmouth, Cape Cod,
Massachusetts 02673
Telephone: 508-771-3433
Toll-free Reservations:
1-800-9-MANOR-9 (1-800-962-6679)
FAX: 508-790-1186
(call prior to FAXing)
E-Mail: manorhse@capecod.net
Web Site: www.capecod.net/manorhouse

Proprietors/Hosts:
Liz and Rick Latshaw

77 miles/1-1/2 hours from Boston
77 miles/1-1/2 hours from Providence, Rhode Island

Guestrooms: (6): each with private bath; individually-decorated.

Picket Fence and *Cranberry Bog*: queen or double bed; small sitting area; private bath with shower.

Birdsong, Howling Coyote, Secret Garden, and *Whalewatch*: queen bed; sitting area; private bath with antique tub; some with bay views and/or air conditioning.

Room rates: per night; based on double occupancy; $10 per night discount for single occupancy; $20 per night extra for each additional guest; 10% discount available for extended stays; includes full breakfast served by candlelight; afternoon tea at 4 p.m.

Mid-May through October and all holidays	$88 - $128
November through Mid-May	$68 - $98

Honeymoon/Romantic Getaway Packages, Birthday Bash Packages, and Anniversary Celebration Packages available.

No pets permitted.
Non-smoking property.
Children age 12 and older are welcome.
Open all year.

Member: Professional Association of Innkeepers International
Cape Cod Chamber of Commerce
Yarmouth Chamber of Commerce

Rating: AAA Two Diamond Award (1998);
Three Diamond Award (1999)
Mobil Three-Star Rating (1998)

The Seaflower -
A Bed & Breakfast Inn

"Let the sea air restore you. The Seaflower is your dream of a shore vacation. Stay for a day, a week, dream of staying forever."

— **Knute Iwaszko and Pat O'Keefe, Hosts**

Mr. Muggs and a companion cat were rescued in 1994 from a tavern in Elizabeth, a town in northern New Jersey, and were given names in keeping with where they were found.

Having been raised in a home full of people, Mr. Muggs is quite comfortable with the comings-and-goings of guests. Although Knute Iwaszko and Pat O'Keefe built a cat door into the basement window of the bed & breakfast especially so that the orange tabby could come and go as he pleased, it seems to please him most to sit by the front door and meow for guests to open it.

Because he had grown accustomed to being the inn's only cat, Mr. Muggs initially was not fond of the stray kitten that started to come around the Seaflower. So

Knute and Pat intended to give the newcomer to a guest who was coming the next weekend for that express reason. But when the guest had to cancel their plans, Knute and Pat found themselves with a decision to make.

"It doesn't take much to fall in love with a kitten," Pat said. "He has the softest, thickest fur of any cat I've ever had. He's built for petting!"

"He's now one of the bright spots of our inn," Pat added.

He's also mellowed somewhat from his younger days, when this silver tabby would "drive Mr. Muggs crazy with his boundless energy and antics." In fact, that's how he got his name.

Mr. Muggs

The Seaflower is a 1907 Dutch Colonial within a half block of the Atlantic Ocean and the Jersey Shore boardwalk. The beach is a definite drawing card for walking, wave riding, sunning, or moonlight strolls. But according to Knute and Pat, there's much more to a shore vacation or week-end getaway than simply the water. The Belmar-area offers antique hunting, tennis, golf, surf and deep sea fishing, dancing, gambling, as well as exploring local historic sites.

"He was such a pest, we named him Pesto," Knute said. "But then it didn't seem quite fair that Mr. Muggs had a title, so we gave Pesto the title of Señor."

Señor Pesto also can occasion-ally make a pest of himself around guests.

"He's friendly with the guests as long as they understand they are at the Seaflower *to wait on him*," Knute said, adding that the inn's policy is quite the opposite. They pride themselves *on pampering their guests.*

Señor Pesto

In addition to being the resident cats at the Seaflower, Mr. Muggs and Señor Pesto have other things in common: they love to eat and sleep, and they try to sneak into the guestrooms, which are technically off-limits.

Even though the Seaflower is close to everything a guest would want, pampering by the inn's staff is what every guest appreciates.

"Be pampered by our caring staff, and relax while someone else spoils you with a special breakfast," Pat said.

Pat also noted that the b & b's guests are becoming more health-conscious, and as always, the Seaflower is giving its guests exactly what they want.

"Low-cholesterol and low-fat breakfasts with lots of fresh fruits and vegetables seem to suit us all," said Pat.

Especially when it's swimsuit season by the seashore...

The Seaflower -
A Bed & Breakfast Inn

110 9th Avenue
Belmar, New Jersey 07719-2302
Telephone: 732-681-6006
FAX: --
E-Mail: --
Web Site: www.bbianj.com/seaflower

Proprietors/Hosts:
Knute Iwaszko and Pat O'Keefe

60 miles/1-1/4 hours from Atlantic City, New Jersey
50 miles/1-1/2 hours from Philadelphia
50 miles/1-1/2 hours from New York City

Guestrooms: (5) Doubles: each with private bath and ceiling fan. (1) Sunflower Suite: private bath, ceiling fan, two rooms, an alcove bed with ocean view.

Room/suite rates: per night; includes full, multi-course breakfast served in the breakfast room; beach passes; and private parking.

May 1 to Mid-June	$80
Mid-June to Mid-September	$80, midweek; $130, weekends
Mid-September - Oct. 31	$80

No pets permitted.
Smoking permitted only on front porch.
Children over age 9 are welcome.
Open May through October only.

Member: Bed & Breakfast Innkeepers Association
                of New Jersey (charter member)

The Albert Stevens Inn
& Cat's Garden

"When you stay with us, your key unlocks quiet, calm, and sanity, but locks out congestion and tourist frenzy. Here, you'll find two hard-working individuals who escaped the corporate world for a life now dedicated to nurturing and balancing nature."

— Diane and Curt Diviney Rangen, Hosts

Billy became an integral part of the Rangen family six years before Diane and Curt purchased The Albert Stevens Inn & Cat's Garden. It didn't take long for his reputation to precede him as prospective guests would call the inn to be sure Billy was the official greeter in advance of making their reservation.

It was Billy's past that laid the foundation for the Cat's Garden. Billy had been hit by a car and the Rangens nursed him back to health.

"Growing strong and confident, Billy has been in charge of our family ever since the head bandage was removed," Diane recalled. "He is gentle but very protective of his home and cat clan. He is a trusted friend and excellent judge of character."

The Cat's Garden is the cats' own retreat, a private area where they receive unlimited affection and attention from the Rangens, guests of The Albert Stevens Inn, as well as those visitors who experience the authentic Victorian High Tea in the garden and the house tour. Supported by the contributions of the afternoon tea, these felines receive the food, water, shelter, medical attention, and love that otherwise would be lacking from their lives.

Guests can visit the Cat's Garden after breakfast as well as at tea time. Those guests not staying at the inn can make reservations for teas served on Thursdays

Billy

and Sundays at 4 p.m. (Eastern Time). Advance reservations also are necessary for guests planning to attend the Christmas Cats-travaganza served weekends Thanksgiving to Christmas.

"It is our hope that the Garden not only will provide funding to care for the Greater Cape May-area cats without homes, but also will provide an environment where they can be appreciated for the extraordinary creatures that they are," Curt said.

None of the Cat's Garden cats have access to the inn, but instead reside in the Cat's Garden with their own heated cat house where they can sleep and eat undisturbed; pond stocked with fish (strictly for entertainment); private eating area; and of course, privy. To provide protection, the Cat's Garden has a cat guard and a six-foot privacy fence.

Under Diane's direction, the garden is landscaped with hundreds of plants and herbs.

"We'd like to think we have built a place of leisure for our cats, where they too are on vacation from the troubles of the world," Diane said. "At last count, we had 42 cats. This is more cats than sane people admit to owning, but we are sane and all our cats are loved and treasured. Having so many cats as well as human companions has given us a world of richness."

Since these cats range in age from under 12 months to 15 years, the stories abound. **Derek** was born in June 1998 to a feral mother who abandoned him at six days old.

Derek

Since that day, Diane hand-raised him. **Mickey** and **Martha** were born in the Cat's Garden in August 1997 to Olivia, a pure black domestic shorthair. Ever since a guest discovered them snuggled together under a pine tree, Mickey and Martha have been people-oriented and are among the Cat's Garden lap cats.

Martha & Mickey

The next thing Diane knew, the gull had taken flight, with Luke still hanging on! As the gull continued its climb, Diane and Curt could only watch and pray and try and control their hysterics. Then the seagull flipped sideways and Luke rolled off into the mint garden. A few minutes later, he emerged unscathed, proudly carrying a large tail feather in his mouth.

But Diane is particularly fond of the story about **Luke**, which was published in a book entitled, *Cat Caught My Heart*, a compilation of stories of wisdom, hope, and purr-fect love by Michael Capuzzo and Teresa Banik Capuzzo.

According to Diane, Luke carried that tail feather around for the rest of the day for everyone — cats included — to see. Even more significant was that day marked the turnaround in Luke's health.

A winter ago, Luke refused to let Diane tend his sore gums, which resulted in dramatic weight loss. Despite making him as comfortable as possible, Luke's condition would not improve without medication. Then one spring day, Luke "decided to fly" and everything changed.

Finally, Luke was on the road to recovery.

While most of the cats in the Garden scattered when the skies filled with sounds of screaming seagulls, Luke stayed behind, having discovered a gull on the ground. Diane recalled how she watched in horror as Luke leaped and landed "spread-eagle" on this young gull's back.

Luke

Built in 1898 by Dr. Albert Stevens, a Cape May homeopathic medical doctor as a wedding present for his wife, Bessie, this Victorian Queen-Anne classic was restored and became a bed & breakfast in 1980 when the Stevens only child, Vesta, passed on. In 1990, Diane and Curt became the fourth owners and have since restored most of the interior and exterior; upgrades continue virtually non-stop.

Each of the 10 guestrooms has an individual theme and is decorated with period antiques of the Victorian era from 1820 to 1905. Each day begins with a hearty, three-course, Norwegian-style breakfast, and many of the recipes for the breakfasts and the dinners (included in the nightly rate February through April with a two-night stay) can be found in the cookbook entitled, *The Cat's Meow*, published in 1998 by Diane and Curt. The cookbook also is filled with background information on many of the cats that call the Cat's Garden their home, plus delightful sketches and photos of the cats, also taken by the Rangens.

After breakfast, guests meander leisurely to the historical shopping mall, the Cape May Lighthouse, Bird Observatory, beaches, or the Cat's Garden, unique to The Albert Stevens Inn. This non-profit foundation was established in 1992 to provide a safe haven for and to humanely reduce the population of feral cats in the Greater Cape May-area.

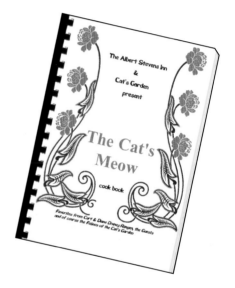

During their stay at The Albert Stevens Inn & Cat's Garden, guests also enjoy walking, biking, hiking, playing golf, horseback riding, and deep sea fishing. The hot tub is available for guest enjoyment October through April.

At day's end, three award-winning restaurants are a mere half-block away, unfortunately not far enough to burn substantial calories for those who dare or care to count.

The Albert Stevens Inn
& Cat's Garden

127 Myrtle Avenue
Cape May, New Jersey 08204
Telephone: 609-884-4717
Toll-free Reservations: 1-800-890-CATS
(NY/NJ/PA Tri-State Area only)
FAX: 609-884-8320
E-Mail: --
Web Site: www.capemaycats.com

Proprietors/Hosts:
Diane and Curt Diviney Rangen

40 miles/1 hour from Atlantic City, New Jersey
120 miles/2 hours from Philadelphia

Guestrooms: (6) rooms: each with private bath; ceiling fan; air conditioning.
(3) Suites: each with private bath; ceiling fan; air conditioning.
(1) Deluxe Suite: private bath; ceiling fans; air conditioning; and kitchenette.

Tapestry: double bed; private bath with shower; first floor.

Study: Lincoln-style queen bed; private bath with tub/shower; first floor.

Web: 1880 double bed; private bath with shower; first floor.

Rose: Victorian double bed; private bath with shower; second floor.

Christmas: Pine queen bed; private bath with tub/shower; second floor.

Glory: Oak double bed; private bath with shower; second floor.

The Suite: king bed; private bath with shower; sitting room with color television; second floor.

Cats Suite: Feather double bed and twin bed; private bath with shower; second floor.

The Tower Suite: Feather queen bed; wicker furniture including twin bed; small refrigerator; features floating staircase; occupies entire third floor.

The Conservatory Suite: queen bed; sunken sitting area with skylight; private bath with shower; full kitchenette with stove and refrigerator; second floor.

Room/suite rates: per night; based on double occupancy; includes full, three-course, Norwegian-style breakfast; continental breakfast available for early risers upon request.

| Rooms/suites | $85 - $175 |

No pets permitted.
Smoking permitted only on open porch.

Member: Chamber of Commerce of Greater Cape May and
        Cape May County Chamber
        Bed & Breakfast Association of Cape May
        Mid-Atlantic Center for the Arts
        Historic Accommodations of Cape May

Glendorn,
A Lodge in the Country

"This historic vacation hideaway, with its attendant sense of privacy and privilege, is now enjoyed by those wanting to pause, take stock, and renew themselves in attentive surroundings."

— **Linda and Gene Spinner, Managers**

According to **Reggie's** "resume," her "employment objective is to secure a reputation as a professional 'hotel' cat and make guests feel at home." And if the guests at Glendorn, A Lodge in the Country, have any say in the evaluation, she definitely has succeeded!

In 1992, two feral kittens were discovered in some brush that was being cleared on the grounds of the Meridian Club, Pine Cay, Turks and Caicos Islands by Reggie Forbes, a marine staff member. Reggie saved the cats. But when one cat didn't make it, Linda and Gene Spinner, who were managers of the property at the time, adopted the other one. They named her Reggie, because she was a fighter and tough, just like the man who had befriended her.

From that moment on, Reggie became the "resident kitten-in-training," which would eventually lead to her position as "professional 'hotel' cat."

"Reggie learned to 'meet-and-greet' by waiting for us to return from work at the Clubhouse," Linda recalled.

From 1993 to 1994, Reggie accompanied Linda and Gene as they traveled extensively in the United States. While traveling via airline and auto and staying in various properties, Reggie grew accustomed to different people, places, and situations.

At the Spinner's next position, Reggie would "host" the guest cocktail reception.

"While the resident cat at Fox Equestrian Ranch in Colorado, Reggie would mingle with the guests during the cocktail hour, often sitting on the bar stool and 'allowing' guests to feed her bits of salmon," Linda said.

In her present "job," Reggie has taken on several duties, including opening the office each morning; greeting guests and inviting them to scratch her tummy; napping and being photographed in the garden; standing guard at the kitchen door; and bidding guests fond farewell. Her access to guest living areas is restricted to the outdoor garden and office reception area. Although she'd like to venture elsewhere, she's learned not to because of some guest's allergies and dislikes.

"She is a very smart cat," Linda said.

At night and when she's "off-duty," Reggie stays in the Manager's Cottage. Here she shares her accommodations with Dorky, an adopted stray that cares for and trusts only Linda and Gene. Because she's not guest-friendly like Reggie, Dorky stays exclusively in or around the Spinner's residence where guests are unlikely to see or meet her.

Reggie

Bounded on two sides by the Allegheny National Forest, Glendorn is an environmentally-sensitive estate of 1,280 acres in northwest Pennsylvania. Built in 1928 by Clayton Glenville "Bondieu" Dorn, a local businessman who developed an innovative process to extract oil from abandoned fields, the lodge was a special place for "his extensive and busy family to come together whenever possible for recreation, learning, and renewal." For five generations, Glendorn was the family retreat for the Dorn family. In 1995, the family opened the estate to the public in order to share its self-restorative powers and unique recreational facilities.

Each of the estate's unique cabins and suites features at least one wood-burning fireplace — some have two or three. In all, 41 fireplaces grace the estate, including the two-story fireplace in the main lodge or Big House that burns four-foot logs.

Available on the property and included in the room rate are two rubico clay and one all-weather Omnicourt tennis courts; lakes and streams filled with rainbow, brown and brook trout, bass and bluegill; miles of trails for walking, cross-country skiing, or snowshoeing; bicycles; 60-foot outdoor swimming pool;

gymnasium; and game room with billiards and pool.

Golf, sporting clays, and downhill skiing are available nearby.

Glendorn,
A Lodge in the Country

1032 West Corydon Street
Bradford, Pennsylvania 16701
Telephone: 814-362-6511
Toll-free Reservations: 1-800-843-8568
FAX: 814-368-9923
E-Mail: glendorn@penn.com
Web Site: www.glendorn.com

Owners:
The Dorn Family

Managers:
Linda and Gene Spinner

90 miles/1-1/2-hours from Buffalo, New York
180 miles/4 hours from Cleveland, Ohio
150 miles/4 hours from Pittsburgh, Pennsylvania

Guestrooms: (2)
Suites: (2)
Cabins: (6)

The Balcony Room: queen bed; private bath; $315 per night, single; $375 per night, double.

The Redwood Room: two twin beds (can convert to king bed); private bath; $315 per night, single; $375 per night, double.

The Dorn Suite: living room with fireplace; separate bedroom with queen bed and fireplace; sunporch; private bath with separate tub and shower; $485 per night, single; $545 per night, double.

The Green Suite: sitting area with fireplace; sleeping alcove with queen bed; private bath with separate tub and shower; $385 per night, single; $445 per night, double.

Cabin One: sitting area with fireplace; king bed; private bath; $385 per night, single; $445 per night, double.

Miller Cabin (one bedroom): living area with fireplace and day bed; bedroom with queen bed, wood-burning stove and private bath; screened porch; extra bath; $485 per night, single; $545 per night, double; $645 per night, triple.

Jill's Cabin (one bedroom): living area with fireplace; bedroom with queen bed; private bath; $385 per night, single; $445 per night, double.

The Hutch (one bedroom): living room with fireplace; screened porch with fireplace; bedroom with king bed and fireplace; private bath; $485 per night, single; $545 per night, double.

The Roost (three bedrooms): living area with fireplace; master bedroom with king bed, fireplace, "his" and "her" private baths; second, adult bedroom with king bed, shares bath with bedroom with twin beds; third, adult bedroom with king bed, fireplace, shares bath with bedroom with twin bed; $895 per night, up to four people; $1,125 per night, five or six people; $1,225 per night, seven people; $1,325 per night, eight people.

Guest House on Skipper Lake (four bedrooms): living room with fireplace and lake view; four bedrooms: three with king beds; one with king or twin beds; each bedroom with private bath with separate tub and shower; terry robes and slippers; kitchenette; courtyard hot tub; two bedrooms: $795 per night, two people; $895 per night, three people; $995 per night, four people; three bedrooms: $995 per night, three people; $1,095 per night, four people; $1,195 per night, five people; $1,295 per night, six people; four bedrooms: $1,195 per night, four people; $1,295 per night, five people; $1,395 per night, six people; $1,495 per night, seven people; $1,595 per night, eight people.

Room/suite/cabin rates: per night; includes full breakfast, lunch, and dinner served in the Main House Dining Room; continental breakfast can be delivered to cabins; complimentary beverages.

	Single	Double	Triple
Rooms	$315	$375	—
Suites	$385 - $485	$445 - $545	—
Cabins	$385 - $485	$445 - $545	$645

	Up to 4 people	5 - 6 people	7 people	8 people
Roost Cabin	$895	$1,125	$1,225	$1,325

	Two Bedrooms			Three Bedrooms			
	2 p	3 p	4 p	3 p	4 p	5 p	6 p
Guest House	$795	$895	$995	$995	$1,095	$1,195	$1,295

Four Bedrooms				
4 p	5 p	6 p	7 p	8 p
$1,195	$1,295	$1,395	$1,495	$1,595

Packages available.
The entire Glendorn Estate can be rented for exclusive, private retreats, where children of any age are welcome.

No pets permitted.
Smoking permitted except in Dining Area and Pine Room/Library.
Children over age 12 are welcome.
1999 annual closing: January 3 - February 4; reservations line remains open.

Member: Historic Hotels of America
Independent Innkeepers Association

Past Purr-fect
Bed and Breakfast

"We live on the premises and enjoy our b & b. We are social to our guests and make them feel welcome."

— **Robin and John Trevaskis, Hosts**

Simba, the Lion King, is the official greeter at the Past Purr-fect Bed and Breakfast and will escort guests to their guestroom, if they so desire. The best "tip" you can possibly give Simba is to play catch with him, his favorite pastime.

Simba began his life as the Trevaskis' pet. The family chose him specially because the Maine Coon breed is known to be very friendly. His name was chosen by two children, ages 9 and 11, because the cat's father weighed in at 25 pounds, and they expected his offspring to be equally as "powerful."

"You could actually hear his paws hit the floor," Robin said. "Simba shares the same trait."

Simba also is a strong-willed cat. After being part of the Trevaskis family for only one week, he became sick and they

nearly lost him. But after daily shots and daily doses of TLC, he made a full recovery and is now purr-fectly healthy.

Centrally-located near historic Gettysburg, Lancaster County's Amish farmlands, Baltimore's Inner

Simba

Harbor, Harrisburg, and our nation's capital, the Past Purr-fect Bed and Breakfast is a 100+ year-old Victorian with present day luxuries.

Guests enjoy a morning stroll through scenic Nixon Park, a ride along biking paths, or a variety of other sports, includ-ing golf and fishing. Exploring the local culture and shopping at Lancaster County's factory outlets and antique stores also are popular activities. Back at the b & b, there's a sitting room with television. And for those who prefer to do absolutely nothing, there's always relaxing on the screened-in porch.

Past Purr-fect
Bed and Breakfast

216 North Main Street
Jacobus, Pennsylvania 17407
Telephone: 717-428-1634
FAX: 717-428-2041
E-Mail: pstprb&b@blazenet.net
Web Site: --

Proprietors/Hosts:
Robin and John Trevaskis

30 miles/45 minutes from Gettysburg, Pennsylvania
30 miles/45 minutes from Lancaster, Pennsylvania

Guestrooms: (4): (1) with private bath; (3) with sink only/share baths; each with telephone; decorated in a variety of cat motifs.

Room rates: per night; based on double occupancy; rates are adjust-ed for longer stays; includes full breakfast with homemade baked goods served in the formal dining room.

Rooms $50 - $65

No pets permitted.
Smoking permitted only outside.

Member: White Rose Bed & Breakfast Association/
Chamber of Commerce

Hollileif
Bed & Breakfast

Furguson, a.k.a. Furgy, was about a year-and-a-half old when she and the Butkuses moved to Hollileif. She was Ellen's anniversary present to herself because life hadn't been the same since their cat Vicky had passed on. Ellen had her heart set on a Persian, but despite much advance legwork, when she got to what she thought was the purr-fect pet shop, she was told the kittens were too young for adoption. But this Silver Tabby Exotic Shorthair was ready for a home. Since Vicky had been named for Queen Victoria, Richard suggested that they maintain the Royal Family theme and name the newest addition after Fergie.

Furgy is strictly an indoor cat, and even when a guest inadvertently leaves the door open, she only stares out as if watching television. Guests also are requested to keep their guest-room doors closed so Furgy won't enter. She's quite guest-friendly, although she's afraid of children and boisterous adults. She loves to be the center of attention and will meow, stand on her hind legs, and rub her head against those who ignore her. And if she brings her small foam ball to a guest who's checking in, she'll "cry" if they don't get the message and throw it for her to retrieve.

Furgy was best friends with Danielle. When Danielle lost her battle with cancer, Ellen and Richard tried to find a kitten that Furgy would grow to love.

PHOTO BY GEORGE W. GARDNER

"Although it took several months for Furgy to accept **Jenny**, they now get along but are not as close as Furgy and Danielle were," Ellen said.

Jenny is a Silver Tabby American Shorthair named for Jennyannydots from the hit musical *Cats*, though she is nothing like the cat for whom she was named.

"She has not turned out to be a 'Gumbie' cat. She is very feisty," Ellen added.

Like Furgy, Jenny is kept indoors and is not allowed to mingle with guests in their rooms. Outside of their rooms is another story entirely.

"Jenny is a friendly cat. She is still young and very active and likes to tease the guests," Ellen said. "She loves to be the center of attention and will let you know if she thinks she's not getting her fair share."

Even though Jenny has been part of the Butkuses lives for only a short period of time, Ellen has two favorite stories she likes to share.

"I was alone in the inn, except for Jenny and Furgy. I heard voices, which at first I assumed was a radio. After a minute or two, I realized it was the answering machine," Ellen said. "I walked into the living room to find Jenny sitting on the front desk, next to the answering machine, listening to old messages. She had apparently pressed the 'message play' button!"

Jenny & Furgy

"When I'm doing the laundry, Jenny likes to follow me to the basement through a cat door. When the phone rang, I had to run upstairs to take the call, leaving a basket full of damp clothes," Ellen said. "After I finished talking, I turned around to find Jenny on the living room side of the cat door with a wet undershirt in her mouth. She was tugging at it to pull it through the cat door!"

Richard likes to refer to both Furgy and Jenny as "commuter cats" since he carries them from the carriage house, where they live, to the inn each morning after breakfast has been served.

This romantic respite in the Bucks County countryside is situated on five-and-a-half, parklike acres. In the warm months, Hollileif's spacious grounds are purr-fect for unwinding on a hammock under a shady tree, or a friendly game of volleyball, badminton, croquet, bocce ball, or horseshoes. When the snow falls, the inn's hill is ideal for sledding, and the wood-burning fireplace in the living room is wonderful for snuggling, reading, quiet conversation or reflection.

Rich in Revolutionary War history, the area boasts many historical attractions, cultural activities, gourmet restaurants, and shops — from Peddler's Village to art and antique galleries, boutiques, outlets, auctions and flea markets. The beautiful, gently-rolling scenery can be explored and enjoyed by car, bike, on foot, or even by boat — canoes are available for rent at nearby Tyler State Park. Canoes, motorboats, and sailboats can be rented at Nockamixon State Park, approximately 30 minutes away.

Hollileif
Bed & Breakfast

PHOTO BY GEORGE W. GARDNER

677 Durham Road (Route 413)
Newtown, Pennsylvania 18940
Telephone: 215-598-3100
FAX: --
E-Mail: hollileif@aol.com
Web Site: www.bbhost.com/hollileif

Proprietors/Hosts:
Ellen and Richard Butkus

30 miles/45 minutes from Philadelphia
6 miles/8 minutes from New Hope, Pennsylvania

Guestrooms: (5): each with private bath; air conditioning; (2) have gas fireplaces.

Room rates: per night; includes four-course gourmet breakfast served at individual tables in intimate breakfast room; afternoon refreshments; complimentary sherry and brandy.

Monday - Thursday, excluding holidays and holiday periods	$85 - $110
Friday - Sunday, plus holiday and holiday periods	$115 - $160

No pets permitted.
Smoking permitted only outdoors.
Reservations recommended.

Member: Professional Association of Innkeepers International
          Bed & Breakfast Inns of Bucks and Hunterdon Counties
          Bucks County Conference and Visitors Bureau
          Pennsylvania Travel Council

Rating: AAA Two Diamond Award (1998)
          Mobil Two-Star Rating (1998)

The Churchill House Inn

"Churchill House, truly an inn for all seasons, is pleased to be your home away from home for a perfect vacation. We invite you to come, relax, and enjoy that special magic that is Vermont."

— **Linda and Richard Daybell, Hosts**

Audrey is relatively new to innkeeping since Linda and Richard Daybell are the new innkeepers at The Churchill House Inn. But she has been part of the Daybell's lives for the past 12 years, having been a birthday gift to Linda to "replace her human child who was about to go away to college."

Named for Linda's late mother Audrey, this domestic shorthair had "world privileges" prior to moving to the inn. When outdoors, she enjoys hunting, smelling the flowers, and chasing bugs. Inside, Audrey loves to play with pencils and corks, all of which helps to create a healthy appetite for another favorite pastime — eating.

Built by the Churchill Family in 1872, this farmhouse has been welcoming travelers for well over a century.

Each of its nine guestrooms is decorated with a blend of original furnishings, antique pieces, eccentricities of early Vermont architecture, colorful stenciling, and modern bedding with antique bedspreads piled with pillows.

For guests who simply want to relax, the inn offers two sitting areas, enclosed porch, as well as an outdoor pool and sauna. For walkers, hikers, mountain bikers, and cross-country skiers, the Moosalamoo area of the Green Mountain National Forest literally begins at the edge of the property. Guests also can take advantage of the marked trails for birdwatch-

Audrey

ing, berry picking, as well as looking for moose.

The Churchill House Inn is an ideal base from which to tour the state. Within an hour's drive of the inn there's Middlebury College, Fort Ticonderoga, the Vermont Marble Exhibit, the New England Maple Museum, the Shelburne Museum, the quaint town of Woodstock, the

Vermont Teddy Bear factory, and Ben & Jerry's ice cream factory.

Nearby Lake Dunmore is a popular swimming beach, as well as a great spot for canoeing, sailing, and windsurfing.

Also nearby, guests will find delightful small shops — everything from crafts to factory outlets.

The Churchill House Inn

Route 73 East
RR# 3 Box 3265
Brandon, Vermont 05733
Telephone: 802-247-3078
FAX: --
E-Mail:
innkeeper@churchillhouseinn.com
Web Site: www.churchillhouseinn.com

Proprietors/Hosts:
Linda and Richard Daybell

200 miles/3-1/2 hours from Boston
262 miles/4-3/4 hours from New York City
142 miles/3 hours from Montreal, Canada

Guestrooms: (9): each with private bath.

Room rates: per person based on double occupancy; add $25 per night for single occupancy; no charge for children under age 5; children ages 5 - 12 are half-price when sharing a room with adults; includes full breakfast and lunch.

Daily	$85 - $95 per person
Three-Day Getaway	$195 - $240 per person
Five-Day Holiday	$300 - $360 per person

No pets permitted.
Smoking permitted only outside.

The Lilac Inn

"Return to the grandeur of a 1909 Vermont summer cottage...our home is a welcome respite to a world of beauty, elegant comfort, amiable conversation, and quiet relaxation, all within a five-minute walk to the unhurried, unspoiled, unforgettable town of Brandon."

— Melanie and Michael Shane, Hosts

Both of the Shane's cats were their pampered pets before they became inn cats.

It took time for **White Darling**, found at a construction site, to outgrow her tendency to bite and claw. But this pure white cat with blue eyes that the Shanes refer to as an Alley-Siamese, is now content to curl up in the inn's office during the day because she often roams the open guestrooms at night. She seems partial to business travelers who may also be burning the midnight oil.

White Darling, a.k.a. Love Child and Sweetness, has found a special calling: she has become the alarm system for a hearing-impaired guest.

"The guest originally asked us to wake him with flashing lights," Michael said. "Now, he just takes the cat and she wakes him with her movement."

Sebastian, a Chocolate Point Himalayan, formerly belonged to one of the Shane's grown children. He loves to show off his fabulous appearance, but he's as intelligent as he is gorgeous.

"Sebastian is the smartest cat," Michael said. "We used to wrap his toy mice in tissue paper. After he played with the un-wrapped mice, he would re-wrap them in the same paper!"

Sebastian loves to greet both new and returning guests, and enjoys his guestroom privileges.

When Sebastian was pictured in an article about The Lilac Inn, Michael said they received any

White Darling

PHOTO BY KINDRA CLINEFF

about 40 a year for a guest list of two to 250. Both the glass-enclosed ballroom and the grounds, which feature extensively-landscaped gardens, flower-lined cobblestone patios, and ponds, are sentimental favorites for wedding couples.

Even when the chef is putting the finishing touches on a picture-purr-fect wedding reception, he's preparing the

Sebastian

number of calls wanting to know his breed and where they might find a breeder. And it goes without saying, their inquiries about Sebastian were followed by calls to make reservations.

Both Sebastian and White Darling get along with the Shane's four Pug dogs, who spend their time in the owner's residence.

The Lilac Inn is Brandon, Vermont's largest mansion, designed by Chicago Architect George Perkins for Albert Farr, a Brandon native who made his fortune as a Chicago banker. Situated on one of the most beautiful avenues in the state, the inn features six wood-burning fireplaces; art and mementos from the owners' world travels, and a 10,000-volume library.

The Lilac Inn is renowned for its remarkable weddings, hosting

inn's award-winning, contemporary New England cuisine. The inn serves dinner Wednesday through Saturday as well as brunch on Sunday for its guests and local patrons.

Walking-, hiking-, and biking-enthusiasts will find many opportunities just steps away. Depending upon the season, exercise options within a mile include tennis, golf, horseback riding, and ice skating. Downhill skiing is a 30-minute drive, while both cross-country skiing and fishing are 20 minutes away by car.

History buffs know that Brandon was a stop on the underground railroad; the area has many Civil War sites.

There's also antique shops and galleries galore in and around Brandon.

The Lilac Inn

53 Park Street
Brandon, Vermont 05733
Telephone: 802-247-5463
Toll-free Reservations: 1-800-221-0720
FAX: 802-247-5499
E-Mail: lilacinn@sover.net
Web Site: www.lilacinn.com

Proprietors/Hosts:
Melanie and Michael Shane

150 miles/3 hours from Boston
125 miles/2-1/4 hours from Albany, New York

Guestrooms: (9): each with private bath.

Bridal Suite: four-poster, pewter/silver canopy bed; whirlpool tub; floor-length mirrors; make-up mirror; and fireplace.

Room/suite rates: per night; includes full, multi-course breakfast.

Rooms and Suite	$115 - $250

No pets permitted.
Non-smoking property.

Member: Heart of Vermont Lodging Association
Vermont State Chamber of Commerce

Rating: AAA Three Diamond Award (1998)
Mobil Three-Star Rating (1998)

Manchester Highlands Inn

Having a resident cat on a bed & breakfast, inn, or hotel web page is becoming somewhat commonplace, but having his name as part of the e-mail address could just be the cat's meow!

When you want to reach the Manchester Highlands Inn via e-mail, it's humphrey@high-landsinn.com, for **Humphrey**, a Maine Coon that Patricia and Robert Eichorn adopted when he was four-years-old. The Eichorns found Humphrey at the local animal shelter after their cat passed away.

Humphrey loves being an inn cat, and his feelings are reciprocated.

"Humphrey loves our guests and all the attention, not to mention the presents, treats, and Christmas cards he receives from them," Patricia said.

Humphrey's following and reputation even extends across the Atlantic Ocean.

"When Humphrey, the Prime Minister's cat at 10 Downing Street, disappeared, a reporter for a British newspaper called the inn!" Patricia said.

Humphrey will visit with guests in their rooms when invited. He also enjoys spending time outdoors, eating, sleeping, and posing for photos, many of which are taken at the inn's Saturday evening wine-and-cheese hour where he "entertains" the guests.

Humphrey

PHOTO BY ROBERT EICHORN

One of the most popular times to visit the Manchester Highlands Inn is fall foliage when the sugar maples turn the countryside red and gold. The winter attracts both novice and expert skiers since the Stratton and Bromley ski areas are just minutes from the inn's door, offering downhill and cross-country skiing.

Not to be outdone by other resident cats, Humphrey does have his own page on the Manchester Highlands' web site, as well as his own guestbook.

If you want to escape from the crowds yet remain close to the action, then look no further than the Manchester Highlands Inn. Often found curled up on the sofa, Humphrey, the resident cat, has the right idea when it comes to relaxing and enjoying all that this inn and its surroundings have to offer.

Each of the 15 guestrooms recently has been refurbished with feather beds, down comforters, and lace curtains. The furnishings are Country Victorian antiques and reproductions.

Spring is ideal for fly fishing the famous Battenkill, canoeing, hiking, or biking the backroads. Among the summer activities are golf, tennis, croquet on the inn's lawn, relaxing by the outdoor pool, or rocking on the porch and watching the sunset over Mt. Equinox.

Throughout the year, guests relax or mingle in the living room, wicker room, game room with its pool and ping-pong tables, or the pub room for a friendly game of darts or to enjoy the ambiance created by the stone fireplace.

Manchester also is known for its shops (antique, boutique, and high-end factory outlets), galleries, and fine restaurants.

Manchester Highlands Inn

P.O. Box 1754
Highland Avenue
Manchester Center, Vermont 05255
Telephone: 802-362-4565
Toll-free Reservations: 1-800-743-4565
FAX: 802-362-4028
E-Mail: humphrey@highlandsinn.com
Web Site: www.highlandsinn.com
Proprietors/Hosts:
Patricia and Robert Eichorn

155 miles/3 hours from Boston
125 miles/2-1/2 hours from Hartford, Connecticut
200 miles/4 hours from New York City

Guestrooms (15): each with private bath.

Room rates: per night; based on double occupancy; $20 per extra person; $10 extra during foliage season and holiday periods; $20 less for single occupancy, Sunday - Thursday; off-season, mid-week, and corporate rates available; inquire about rooms that accommodate children and corresponding rates; includes full breakfast with plenty of Vermont maple syrup; breakfast can be delivered to guestroom upon request; afternoon tea; and home-baked afternoon snacks.

Rooms $105 - $145

Dinner available for parties of eight or more with prior arrangement. Full liquor license.

No pets permitted.
Smoking permitted only outside.

Member: Professional Association of Innkeepers International
New England Innkeepers Association
Vermont Chamber of Commerce
Vermont Lodging and Restaurant Association

Cheeca Lodge

Cheeca Cat, so named by Cheeca Lodge Security Director John Yonitch because she was born on the property in 1988, has been adopted by *all* of the hotel's employees who ensure she wants for nothing, including her signature black-and-white beaded collar.

"Basically, she is an adopted stray, but she adopted us," John said.

After she had her first — and only — litter (proudly selecting the courtyard of the main lodge to give birth), she was spayed. While the vet confirmed she's a black domestic shorthair, many cat-savvy guests insist she has Bombay in her.

Cheeca Cat only has access to public areas, which is fine with her since she prefers the courtyard — except during thunderstorms, that is. John recalled a particularly violent one swept through the Keys in the early 1990s. The staff was busy with arriving guests and didn't notice Cheeca Cat's pleas to come inside for shelter. So she took matters into her own paws, so to speak.

When someone opened the courtyard door to the lobby, Cheeca Cat raced past the Australian parakeet cages, jumped on the reception desk, meowed loudly, then jumped down, making a beeline for shelter in the reservations office. Having observed this, one of the guests exclaimed, "I've heard of express check-out, but that was express check-in!"

Cheeca Cat loves to loaf in the laid-back elegance of Cheeca Lodge or catch some Florida rays while catnapping on a luggage cart. Despite her wonderful disposition, Cheeca Cat doesn't like anyone except John to pick her up and hold her. However, she will let guests, kids included, pet her. But when she's had enough attention for the day, she makes herself scarce.

"She is very happy and content being Cheeca Cat," John added.

 At Mile Marker 82, Cheeca Lodge is the centerpièce de résistance of the Florida Keys. This 27-acre resort offers 203 oversized guestrooms and suites; two freshwater swimming pools; a saltwater lagoon; six nightlit tennis courts; a Jack Nicklaus-designed, par-3, nine-hole golf course (which doubles as the helipad); an enviable 1,100-foot stretch of private beach; a 525-foot lighted pier ideal for fishing, daydreaming, and dramatic sunrises and sunsets; as well as three restaurants to satisfy every mood and taste. There's roomservice as well as a catering department that caters to group needs from 10 to 180.

The property was among the first to be ecologically-conscientious and environmentally-aware. Camp Cheeca, the hotel's program for children ages six to 12, also led the industry with its focus on education as well as entertainment. Kids and grown-ups alike can learn to snorkel, parasail, windsurf, sail, scuba dive, deep sea fish, backcountry fish, or reef fish, since Islamorada is the world-renowned sport-fishing capital of the world.

Cheeca Cat

Both non-shoppers and those who want to get a jump on their holiday gift-giving will find Cheeca Lodge's boutique filled with unique items that are fun, bright, and colorful — and won't be found anywhere else. The shop features handcrafted works and one-of-a-kind designs by local artisans.

And for those who just want to enjoy the peace and quiet confines of their room, all of Cheeca Lodge's accommodations were completely-remodeled and refurbished in December 1997. Barefoot elegance abounds indoors and out.

Cheeca Lodge

Mile Marker 82
P.O. Box 527
Islamorada, Florida 33036
Telephone: 305-664-4651
Toll-free Reservations: 1-800-327-2888
FAX: 305-664-2893
E-Mail: cheecalodg@aol.com
Web Site: www.cheeca.com

Vice President & General Manager:
Herbert Spiegel

75 miles/1-1/2 hours from Miami
82 miles/1-1/2 hours from Key West

Guestrooms: (139) rooms: each with telephones; color television with video cassette player; private bath; air conditioning; ceiling fan; and fully-stocked mini-bar.

(63) suites: each with telephones; color television with video cassette player; private bath; air conditioning; ceiling fan; fully-stocked mini-bar; full kitchen; living room with sleeper sofa; private, screened-in balcony.

Presidential Suite: telephones; color television with video cassette player; private bath with oversized whirlpool tub; air conditioning; ceiling fan; fully-stocked mini-bar; marble floors; full kitchen; living room with sleeper sofa; private, oceanfront, screened-in balcony.

Room/suite rates: per night; based on single or double occupancy.		
	Summer (4/22/98 - 12/22/98)	Winter (12/23/98 - 4/21/99)
Rooms	$185 - $430	$295 - $650
Suites	$285 - $675	$400 - $1,500
Presidential Suite	$850 - $1,385	$2,100

No pets permitted.

Smoking permitted only in designated guestrooms and
common areas.

Reservations recommended.

Management: Coastal Hotel Group
Member: Small Luxury Hotels and Resorts of the World
Rating: AAA Four Diamond Award (1998)

Blue Parrot Inn

"We are a quiet, relaxed, and friendly house. Year-round, the Parrot's little bit of paradise is ideal for lazy days, crazy nights on the town, and a world of wonderful memories."

— **Frank Yaccino and Larry Rhinard, Hosts**

With six fabulous felines, it may take a while to figure out who's who, especially since they have acquired a nickname or two or three along the way. **Cleo** is at least 13 years old because she had considered the Blue Parrot home for some 10 years already when Frank Yaccino and Larry Rhinard acquired the inn in 1995. At the time she was known as Tiberius (a previous owner named each of his cats

Cleo

after a Roman Emperor). When they discovered the brown mackeral tabby's true gender, the name Cleopatra was chosen because she was as close to being a Roman Empress as anyone.

"Cleo is indeed the Queen of our little pride," Larry said.

Much to the disappointment of some guests, Cleo chooses with whom she wishes to sleep. According to Larry, after she has identified her "mark," she treats the prospective "bedmates" with undue and unsolicited affection.

Betty

"If their door is closed in her face, Cleo will sit immediately outside the door and howl," Larry said. "To our knowledge, Cleo has not yet been refused! Cleo is very guest-friendly and manipulative. She is a cat."

For those guests who can't wait to meet Cleo, a.k.a. Cleesey, check out the Blue Parrot's web page.

Like Cleo, **Betty** had been living at the Blue Parrot when Larry and Frank bought the property. Unlike Cleo, however, she did not have a Roman Emperor's name and would never set a paw in a guestroom, although she is very friendly with the guests *when she is around.* That is the operative phrase.

"Betty, a black-and-white domestic shorthair, is a myste- rious cat," said Frank. "We do not know how or where she spends her time, although we suspect she has a boyfriend at the adjoining guesthouse. She has been observed lounging by his pool and sitting on his veranda."

Ah, the grass is always green- er... Betty also responds to Betty Boop, Booper, and Boop- adoop, when she's around, that is.

One day, **Lady** showed up at the Blue Parrot as a frightened, wild cat. To this day, she won't allow anyone to touch her, although this black-and-white "Key West Stumpie" gives very fond looks with her eyes.

Frank and Larry were the first to name the "Key West Stumpies" because these cats are born with no tails.

Lady

"We do not know if a Manx gene has been intro- duced onto the island or if this taillessness is another mutation," Frank said. "Like the Isle of Man, Key West is an island and there is much inbreeding in the cat population."

Lily

Because all attempts to lure her out from under the porches and decks failed, and she appeared pregnant at the time, Larry and Frank fed her. Imagine their surprise when two months after her arrival, two kittens about four-months-old emerged.

"Hoping to dispel imaginings of her trampish past, we named her Lady," Larry said.

Lady, who appears to be between three and five years old, spends much of her time lounging around the pool area. Another favorite pastime is to run and jump with her "kids."

Lily was the first of Lady's kittens to emerge from under the deck. She was so refined and graceful that they selected Lily as her name. She's also picked up the nickname of Hoover.

"We have a British housekeeper who calls a vacuum a generic 'Hoover®,'" said Frank. "Our other housekeeper has applied this name to Lily since she 'sucks' up all food in her path."

Although this year-and-a-half old gray-and-white has a full tail, she is genetically a Stumpie. She loves to be petted, and especially likes guests who rub her tummy, but she will not venture into the guestrooms.

She also has a fascination for — rather than a fear of — water. One of her favorite games is to push the nuts that fall from the palm trees into the water. She watches intently as they swirl around and slowly sink to the bottom. One day, she apparently decided to try and get a closer look.

"Fortunately, she did not swirl and sink but swam vigorously to the ladder and climbed out as she must have seen countless guests do before her," Larry said. "She then made a mad dash around the deck area and stopped abruptly with a look of humiliation on her face."

To the best of their knowledge, she hasn't repeated that stunt.

Lila is Lily's litter mate, if not her soul mate, as she too has a thing for water. She loves to come to the edge of the pool

Lila

when Larry and Frank are taking a dip.

"She wants us to pat her with our wet hands until she is completely soaked," Larry said.

While Lila is frequently shy around guests, she is Larry's little helper and is always there to supervise when he's gardening or doing outside maintenance. "She is very striking and can

get by *on cute*, but she is a smart little cat," Larry said.

In keeping with the "L" tradition of her mother and sister, she was christened Lila. However, one of the guests referred to her as "Bunnybutt" since she has a pompon for a tail. She also is known as Miss Butt, Buttsker, Lila S., Butt, and Lilabutt.

Sly was the third of Lady's kittens to introduce himself, but since he is about six months younger, he is from a different litter. This black-and-white stumpie with about four inches of a tail so reminded Frank of the famous Sylvester that he named him Sly. His other names include Slippery Sly, Baby Sly, Sly-bucket, and Mister Bucket.

"Frank also began calling him 'Mr. Bucket' as a contradiction to Mrs. Bucket, pronounced by her as Bouquet, of the English TV series," Larry said.

Sly is sometimes outgoing and friendly; other times, he's aloof, but never goes into the guestrooms. Sly always seems to

Sly

Key West also is a cat-friendly island, especially in the historic Old Town-area, where the Blue Parrot Inn is located.

"Many cats are held in common by the community and cared for as such," said Larry. "There is an ongoing spaying and neutering effort of which we are a part. All six of the Blue Parrot's resident cats have been spayed or neutered."

The Blue Parrot Inn was built in 1884 by Walter C. Maloney, author of the first history of Key West. To experience the "Key West frame of mind," stroll down the side streets or take a bike and tool around town. If you enjoy the water, there's sailing, scuba diving, snorkeling, windsurfing, parasailing, jet skiing, kayaking, and swimming. Tennis and golf are available nearby as well. Then unwind in the inn's outdoor, freshwater heated pool, known by guests as a "big warm bathtub." Guests who desire a complete tan will appreciate the clothing optional sundeck, which has a separate access and is completely secluded from those who are more modest.

have an expression of wonderment on his face as if the world is full of surprises.

Wonder what else we can learn from our cat companions!

The Blue Parrot Inn combines the best of both worlds — a quiet, secluded setting with lush tropical foliage in the heart of Key West with its world-class shopping, dining and clubs, water sports, history, and unique location. With the Gulf of Mexico on one side of the road and the Atlantic Ocean on the other, Key West and the Florida Keys are the only car-accessible islands in the Caribbean.

Since cats rule the roost here, the only other "animals" that guests will encounter are many decorative blue parrots.

Blue Parrot Inn

916 Elizabeth Street
Key West, Florida 33040
Telephone: 305-296-0033
Toll-free Reservations: 1-800-231-BIRD (2473)
Fax: --
E-Mail: --
Web Site: www.blueparrotinn.com

Proprietors/Hosts:
Frank Yaccino and Larry Rhinard

155 miles/3-1/2 hours from Miami

Guestrooms: (10): each has distinctive theme/decor.
All rooms include telephone; cable television; private bath; air
conditioning; and ceiling fan; most rooms have refrigerators.

Room rates: per night; based on single or double occupancy;
includes expanded, continental buffet breakfast served poolside.

	Summer & Fall	Winter & Spring
Double	$70, $80, or $90	$105, $115, or $120
Queen	$105	$140
Double & Twin	$110	$145
Double/Double	$120	$165

No pets permitted.
Smoking permitted in guestrooms/anywhere on property.
Children over age 16 are welcome.
Handicapped accessible.
Reservations encouraged.

Member: Key West Innkeepers Association
         Key West Hotel & Motel Association
         InnRoute

Rating: AAA Two Diamond Award (1998)
         Superior Florida Keys Lodging

The Jekyll Island Club Hote

"A supreme standard of comfort, exclusivity, and service, once demanded by the millionaires of yesteryear, are offered to you today at The Jekyll Island Club Hotel."

— Kevin Runner, General Manager

In the summer of 1997, a fashionable, black-and-white kitty with lovely markings strolled into Café Solterra and "asked" for tuna, so the story goes. Immediately smitten with her, guests who were dining there at the time obliged her craving, ordering tuna on a freshly-baked croissant. Apparently, the cuisine was just to her liking, because she decided to stay.

The cat became known as **Jekyll**, in honor of Sir Joseph Jekyll, for whom the exclusive barrier island was named. That, however, was before the staff discovered "he" should have been named "Ms. Jekyll."

Given her introduction to the hotel, it didn't take long for Jekyll to ingratiate herself with guests and staff alike and to make herself purr-fectly at home.

"Guests admire her youth and beauty. She's somewhat shy, but has a steady, wide-eyed gaze," explained Sue Andersson, hotel spokesperson.

"Jekyll is an outdoor cat who actually prefers the veranda, year-round, to any indoor haunt — with one exception," Sue said. "She visits the hotel's flower shop twice each day — mid-morning and late afternoon."

Lest one thinks that Jekyll is partial to cut or exotic flowers, she thoroughly enjoys flora of all kinds. Chances are, if she's off taking a catnap in the sun, there's a flower bed or pot somewhere close by.

Founded in 1886 as an exclusive retreat for the rich and famous like the Morgans, Pulitzers, Rockefellers, and the Vanderbilts, The Jekyll Island Club Hotel features a unique combination of natural beauty and elegant architecture, private amenities and unparalleled personal service. This his-

But sooner than later it's difficult to resist when Chef Bruce Ford prepares gourmet, low-country cuisine in the exquisite Grand Dining Room with its fireplaces, candlelight, live soft music, and view of the Jekyll River. For more casual dining, there's Café Solterra and J.P.'s lounge.

Jekyll

For the ultimate in romance, take a horse-drawn carriage ride through the totally-Victorian, 240-acre historic "millionaire's village." Other ways to unwind and leave the pressures behind include taking a leisurely-stroll or unhurried bike ride along the 22 miles of flat paths through the historic district, wind-

toric hotel is located on a barrier island just six miles off the Georgia coast and is accessible by a causeway.

Guests come to the hotel to be pampered. Accommodations include 134 guestrooms and suites, many with whirlpool tubs purr-fect for soaking away one's cares. In-room dining is available for those who want to keep the world at bay — if only for a little while.

ing one's way along the beach, through the maritime forest, and by the marsh. Let chef prepare a gourmet lunch and make a day of it.

Other ways to enjoy the out-of-doors include 63 holes of championship golf only a mile away (three, 18-hole courses and one, nine-hole course); swimming or lounging around the nearby Olympic-size, heated outdoor pool; tennis; horseback riding;

croquet; and inshore and off-shore fishing. Serious and window-shoppers alike will appreciate the convenience of 12 unique shops, located at or near the hotel, including the property's own gift shop that features sportswear, beach towels, and other items with the Club logo.

The surrounding area is replete with history as well, including Cumberland Island; Fort King George; Fort Frederica; and Hofwyl-Broadfield Plantation.

A National Historic Landmark, The Jekyll Island Club Hotel was the site where the Federal Reserve System was conceived. The first trans-Atlantic telephone call was made from the hotel back in 1915.

The Jekyll Island Club Hotel

371 Riverview Drive
Jekyll Island, Georgia 31527
Telephone: 912-635-2600
Toll-free Reservations: 1-800-535-9547
FAX: 912-635-2818
E-Mail: --
Web Site: www.jekyllclub.com

General Manager:
Kevin Runner

60 miles/1 hour from Jacksonville, Florida
280 miles/5-1/2 hours from Atlanta

Guestrooms: (117): each with private bath; many baths have large whirlpool tubs; many rooms have fireplaces.

(16) Suites: each with private bath; many baths have large whirlpool tubs; many suites have fireplaces.

Presidential Suite: intimate Victorian parlor with wood-burning fireplace opens onto spacious bedroom with wood-burning fireplace; private bath with whirlpool tub and Victorian chaise lounge; spiral staircase leads to turret with antique telescope for stargazing; river and croquet lawn view.

Room/suite rates: per night.

	11/29/98 - 03/04/99	03/05/99 - 08/23/99
Guestrooms	$89 - $159	$125 - $209
Suites	$149 - $179	$199 - $229
Presidential Suite	$229	$279

Packages available; meal plans (American, Modified American, or European) also available.

No pets permitted.
Designated non-smoking floors; food-and-beverage outlets
   are non-smoking.

Member: Historic Hotels of America

Marshall House
Bed & Breakfast Inn

"Thousands of guests have passed through our doors and have enjoyed storytelling time, the whistle of the train, and the captivating view which all make for a unique experience. All guests that come as strangers leave as friends."

— Ruth and Jim Boylan, Hosts

Lady was the first resident cat at the Marshall House, having moved with the Boylans to North Carolina from Florida, where Ruth and Jim were residing. Lady came to live with them when she was just about a year old.

Since she had grown up with warm weather, Lady was accustomed to being outdoors. She initially wanted no part of the b & b, so Ruth and Lady came to an "understanding" that she could stay on the porch. That worked well until one night when it was raining cats and dogs, and Ruth let her dogs out of the backyard pen. They immediately chased Lady up the street.

"She was gone for almost a week and I was sure we had lost her," Ruth said. "After her return, she stayed in one of the rooms, and for about 10 days sat in the windowsill watching the world go by. Then, she just ventured back out, resuming her usual place on the porch like nothing had ever happened."

Now that she's getting older, she only goes out occasionally. She much prefers to sleep on a table behind Ruth's computer or lie on her desk when she's doing paperwork, a position that

Lady

Bashful

many of the other cats seem to enjoy as well. Unless a guest specifically requests one of the cats to join them in their guestroom, Ruth said she encourages the cats to enjoy the other rooms of the Marshall House.

Ruth and Jim considered it the ultimate compliment and the most unique anniversary present when Prissy, a former stray that the Boylans took in from the cold even before they realized she was pregnant, gave birth to **Dusty** and **Bashful** and four other kittens in their bed, on their sixteenth anniversary. (Prissy is no longer with the Boylans; three kittens found good homes elsewhere, and the fourth disappeared, which is why Ruth insists that Dusty stay in at night, though he does venture out during the days.)

Given how he came into this world, it's no wonder that Dusty's preferred place, not to mention his favorite thing to do, is sleeping next to Ruth. This solid gray domestic longhair also paws her if she doesn't give him the attention he thinks he deserves.

Dusty is guest-friendly and wonderful with kids. Ruth recalled that several years ago, a group of photographers was staying at the Marshall House while taking pictures around town. When a child who was supposed to be photographed wouldn't stop crying, Ruth had an idea.

"I would call Dusty and allow the child to hold him. All the tears went away," Ruth said. "Dusty is a very special cat. He comes when I call him and is just a love."

Dusty

Bashful got his name because he used to hide as a kitten hoping to avoid his eye medication. He's outgrown his shyness, and has assumed Lady's position as "defender of the porch." Nowadays, he's keeping his eye on a stray that likes the porch as well. Although he's Dusty's brother, Bashful is dark gray with black stripes and looks a lot like a Maine Coon.

Sherlock

"Bashful is a big guy and he knows it," Ruth said. "He keeps an eye on the stray and when he 'gets out of line,' Bashful lets him know who's boss."

Sherlock and **Watson** got their names because as kittens, they kept wandering over to the Marshall House "to investigate." Their owners asked if the Boylans would care for them while they went on vacation and they obliged. When the owners returned, Ruth told them in no

Watson

uncertain terms that she was keeping the cats because she had heard through the grapevine that they hadn't been getting the best care.

These orange domestic shorthairs are quite affectionate and love the attention that guests give them. They tend to spend most of their time outside.

Ruth said she is beginning to think that whoever lives in that particular house isn't meant to have cats. **Blizzard**, a solid

Blizzard

white domestic semi-longhair, started coming over to the Marshall House when his litter mate disappeared.

"Blizzard apparently did not like to be alone and came here to visit," Ruth said. "I kept taking him back to his owners, who would feed him, and then he would immediately come

Daniella and JoJo

saved him, and stays mainly with him. He's also befriended **Daniella**, one of three kittens born to Bandit, who is no longer with the Boylans. JoJo remains somewhat skittish around everyone else, including Ruth, and since he spends most of his time on the inn's third floor, guests aren't as likely to see him as some of the other resident cats.

back over here. Eventually, I stopped taking him back and it was a foregone conclusion that he was our cat."

Blizzard splits his time between indoors and outside. He's likely to be found on the laundry room shelf, on Ruth's lap when she's eating, or on the dining room table. He's friendly with the guests and playful with the other cats, who sometimes misinterpret his playfulness as dominance.

JoJo was one of three feral kittens that meowed for days near the front porch of the Marshall House. Jim enlisted the help of his friend Joe to catch the domestic shorthair, who they discovered was quite sick. As his way of saying thanks, Jim named the kitty after his friend. While the other two kittens were heard, they were never seen.

JoJo, who is solid black except for a white tip on his tail, is forever grateful to Jim for having

It's no wonder that JoJo and Daniella get along so famously since they both would never let guests pet them. While JoJo is Daniella's favorite, she'll occasionally snuggle up to Dusty.

Daniella was named for Daniel Day Lewis who starred in the hit movie, *My Left Foot*. Daniella is a domestic shorthair with tortoiseshell and calico coloring; her left foot is light tan while her right foot is darker.

One of the boys in the neighborhood brought a tabby kitten to the Marshall House because his family was not in a position to keep her. Jim named her **BoBo** because it seemed to fit, and the last name of **Rockefeller** soon followed. Bobo Rockefeller spent the first three months of her time with Ruth and Jim in their quarters, never venturing downstairs. Then one day, the Boylans came

BoBo Rockefeller

home to find a new cat sitting on their living room rug.

"We had a pretty good idea where she came from, but the same neighborhood boy never called to say he left this cat at our house," Ruth said. "Months later I saw him and he said the timing still hadn't been right for him to have a cat, so

Tigger

since we weren't home, he took the liberty of leaving her."

Because this tabby with white feet and white under her chin was so feisty, the Boylans named her **Tigger**. Tigger decided that the third floor was her domain, "evicting" BoBo. It

might have been a blessing in disguise because Bobo has really come into her own once she discovered a world outside the upstairs.

Although BoBo is somewhat friendly with guests, her demeanor can change quickly so Ruth cautions guests to handle her carefully and pet only her head.

Tigger, on the other hand, doesn't allow guests to touch her anywhere. She rarely goes outside, preferring instead to rule the third floor with an iron "claw."

Jasmine and **Casper**, two domestic shorthairs with Siamese in them, belonged to a guest, but when she was ready to leave, Jim invited the cats to stay at the Marshall House permanently because he had become attached to them.

"Since this guest left us, she has moved a half-dozen times, so the cats were much better off here," Ruth said.

Jasmine

Casper

Like Bashful, Casper is quite fond of the porch. He prefers the outdoors, and except for the time he wandered off and stayed away for a week, he has not strayed from the Marshall House. He is skittish and not friendly towards the guests.

Jasmine is not guest-friendly either, yet she loves the Boylan's dog, Tar, a Great Dane/Shepherd mix that weighs in at 117 pounds.

"Jasmine adores Tar. She sits with her whenever possible, even when she's in her pen in the back," Ruth said. "Jasmine must not think I approve because when I see them together, they act like misbehaved kids and Jasmine slinks away."

Tar also has found a following with **Tip**, **DoDo**, and **Gracie**, three tabby kittens born to mama cat, **Angel**, a domestic shorthair so named because she is just an angel.

Actually, during the summer of 1997, a woman rang the doorbell with four "motherless" kittens in hand. She explained to Ruth's friend, Sandy, who was at the b & b at the time, that she had been sent by the sheriff. Despite Sandy's valiant efforts to get to the vet, buy formula, and try to feed the kittens, Ruth was concerned that they wouldn't get the proper nourishment, so she contacted another woman who knew how to care for kittens without a mother.

The next night, Ruth received a call from a distraught woman asking if she had the kittens.

Gracie, DoDo & Tip

She apparently had learned that her tenant had been hiding the kittens and the mother cat in her barn. Having asked her tenant not to go into the barn anymore for fear she might be stealing from her, the tenant thought she had no

Angel

tens to the sheriff, leaving the mother cat behind.

"When the landlady found out what her tenant had done, she made several calls before reaching me," Ruth said. "She was relieved to find we knew the kittens' whereabouts. We convinced her how important it was to reunite the mother cat with her kittens."

At about 10:30 that night, Sandy, Ruth, and Tar ventured out to bring the family together once again.

From that moment on, Tar became a surrogate mother to the kittens.

"When we got home, Tar refused to come out of the car until mama and her kittens came out," Ruth said. "Tar watched intently as we set up a laundry basket, lined it with towels, and placed them in it. When it was all set, the mother cat (Angel) jumped out of the basket and rubbed up to Tar, giving her permission to look at them. Tar then proceeded to

lick them, giving her stamp of approval."

During the weeks that followed, when Tar came up at night, Angel would leave her basket.

"She would let Tar tend the licking and cuddling of the kittens while she took a break," Ruth said.

Ruth said they found a home for one of the kittens, keeping the other three and their mama.

To this day, the kittens snuggle up to Tar.

"They just love her and the feeling is mutual," Ruth said.

Guests at the Marshall House who are also dog lovers enjoy Tar's company as well.

 The Marshall House Bed & Breakfast Inn is filled with antiques and antique furnishings, including collections of tea cups, tea pots, steins, thimbles, bells, and figurines. Among the most priceless of these possessions is a watercolor of Ruth when she was a little girl painted by the famous pianist Liberace. Jim, who is an award-winning fine art sculptor in his own right, displays some of his original works throughout the house, which was built in 1903 by Richard Sharp Smith for

James H. White. The house is listed in the National Register of Historic Places.

Other special features of the house include the four fireplaces and the 50-foot veranda, where guests can relish in the view of the French Board River and the timeless Appalachian Mountains.

For those who want to explore the quaint town of Marshall, depending upon the season, there's walking/hiking in the

Appalachian Trail - Max Patch; fishing; golfing; whitewater rafting; and snow skiing. Top any or all of these activities off with a dip in the warm mineral baths.

Those who enjoy history and historic homes will want to take the 30-minute drive to see Vanderbilt's Biltmore Estate; the Thomas Wolfe home; the Carl Sandburg home; and the Cherokee Indian Reservation.

Marshall House
Bed & Breakfast Inn

100 Hill Street
P.O. Box 865
Marshall, North Carolina 28753
Telephone: 828-649-9205
FAX: 828-649-2999
E-Mail: TWAQ42A@prodigy.com
Web Site: www.geocities.com/
MadisonAvenue/2501/marshallpage.html

Proprietors/Hosts:
Ruth and Jim Boylan

18 miles/30 minutes from Asheville, North Carolina

Guestrooms: (8): (2) with private bath; (6) with shared bath.

James Penland (Room #1): double bed; $30 per night, single; $40 per night, double.

Maud English Ramsey (Room #2): double bed; $30 per night, single; $40 per night, double.

James (J.H.) White (Room #3): brass bed; private bath; $35 per night, single; $47 per night, double.

Robert S. Ramsey (Room #4): two single beds; $30 per night, single; $45 per night, double.

Balsam Tourist Home (Room #5): double bed; $30 per night, single; $40 per night, double.

Pauline Ramsey Ditmore (Room #6): double bed; $30 per night, single; $40 per night, double.

Annie May White (Room #7): two double beds; $30 per night, single; $40 per night, double, one bed; $45 per night, double, two beds; $50 per night, triple; $55 per night, four people.

Leo White (Room #8): queen and single bed; $32 per night, single; $42 per night, double, one bed; $47 per night, double, two beds; $52 per night, triple; $57 per night, four people.

Bessie Lee Penland (Grand Room): large room with double and single bed; cot; private bath with tub and shower; fireplace; private entrance; $45 per night, single; $65 per night, double; $70 per night, triple; $75 per night, four people.

Room rates: per night; $10 extra during October; includes full breakfast in dining room; upon request, breakfast can be delivered to guestroom or served on the porch.

	Single	Double One Bed	Double Two Beds	Triple	Four People
Rooms #1, 2, 5 & 6	$30	$40	—	—	—
Room #3	$35	$47	—	—	—
Room #4	$30	$45	—	—	—
Room #7	$30	$40	$45	$50	$55
Room #8	$32	$42	$47	$52	$57
Grand Room	$45	$65	$65	$70	$75

Pet-friendly.
Smoking permitted.

The Inn at Merridun

J.D. might well be the only resident cat with his own journal. Entitled, *J.D.'s Journal* or *Confessions of the Inn Cat*, the first entry explains how J.D., short for Jefferson Davis, captured the heart of a confirmed dog lover and got his nickname.

Jim Waller was responsible for J.D.'s arrival at the inn back in November 1991. At the time, Peggy Waller had two dogs, and she made it abundantly clear that she wasn't fond of cats. But Jim convinced her that the inn needed a "mouser." The only catch was that it was cold outside and J.D. was quite small. So, he was kept indoors. It took just three days for Peggy to fall in love with "Just A Darn Cat," which she insists is what J.D. originally stood for.

J.D., a domestic shorthair, also answers to J.D. Waller, Munchkins, Love Bug, and Aristocat.

J.D. is allowed in the guestrooms, and will spend entire evenings with some guests who specifically request his company. But when the inn hosts a large function, or guests are allergic or afraid of cats, J.D. stays with the Wallers.

In addition to spending time with guests in their rooms, J.D. enjoys curling up in their laps, playing, sleeping, and gazing out the windows — at the squirrels and four stray cats that always remain outdoors — T.C., Mama Lucy, StarBright, and StarLight.

But despite J.D.'s sometimes pleas, he is not allowed outside. Because he can be persuasive, the Wallers have posted a sign on the door that reads, "I'm not allowed outside even when I beg and whine! J.D. Cat."

Even before J.D.'s picture was prominently placed on the inn's web site, he was establishing quite a following. While Peggy and Jim often receive thank-you notes from guests, J.D. gets goodies, including cat toys and videos.

Sometimes Jim and Peggy wonder whether they are "Just Darn" inn people and J.D. is really in charge!

The Inn at Merridun is an elegant, yet comfortable antebellum mansion that Peggy and Jim are lovingly-restoring to a one-of-a-kind country inn.

Built in 1855-57 by William Keenan and known as the Keenan Plantation, the home was renamed Merridun in 1885 to reflect the three family names that graced this ancestral home — <u>Mer</u>riman, <u>Ri</u>ce, and <u>Dun</u>can.

With retirement from the Navy approaching, Jim and Peggy knew they weren't ready to retire so they began to think about starting a second career. Since they both loved to entertain, enjoyed people, and had fond memories of their escapes to b & b's, they decided to see whether innkeeping really was their next calling.

Although they originally thought they'd find a country farmhouse or Victorian on the west coast, these former easterners returned

J.D.

PHOTO BY RHONDA GREGORY

to their roots when they visualized the potential that Merridun held.

"You will have to come for a visit to see the before pictures," Peggy said. "Often we even forget how far we have come."

"The city officials and the people of Union have been very good to us. We lovingly say that Merridun really belongs to the people of Union; they only graciously allow us to pay the mortgage," Peggy added.

This Greek Revival inn is only a five-minute walk to downtown Union, yet its library, parlors, marbled veranda, and nine acres of wooded grounds give guests little reason to leave until it's time to check out. For those who do venture out, there's bicycling, tennis, golf, horseback riding, fishing, and shopping, all nearby. In addition to the home's own history (it's listed in the National Register of Historic Places), the area boasts many Revolutionary War and Civil War sites.

Culinary memories are an integral part of a guest's stay at The Inn at Merridun. In addition to the evening dessert and beverages and the three-course, country gourmet breakfast (save room for the dessert course), dinner is served most evenings for an additional charge; advance reservations are required.

Somewhere in Peggy's "spare time" she found the time in 1997-98 to publish her first cookbook. Entitled, *Culinary Memories of Merridun, Volume 1: A Collection of Our Most Requested Recipes*, the cookbook includes stories about Merridun, helpful hints from the kitchen, in addition to 140+ recipes. That's not to imply that Peggy is the only chef in the family. Jim is an accomplished cook as well, and has his own newspaper column entitled "Cooking-Inn Style." Looks like writing also runs in the Waller household.

That's probably where J.D. got his passion for the pen!

The Inn at Merridun

An Antebellum Country Inn
100 Merridun Place
Union, South Carolina 29379
Telephone: 864-427-7052
FAX: 864-429-0373
E-Mail: merridun@carol.net
Web Site: www.bbonline.com/sc/merridun/

Proprietors/Hosts:
Peggy and Jim Waller and J.D. Cat

68 miles/1-1/4 hours from Columbia, South Carolina
68 miles/1-1/4 hours from Charlotte, North Carolina

Guestrooms: (5)

Union Square: queen bed; private bath with shower; non-working fireplace; telephone; cable television; terrycloth robes; and hair dryer.

The Senator's Chamber: king bed; private bath with shower; non-working fireplace; telephone; cable television; terrycloth robes; and hair dryer.

The Governor's Gallery: king bed; private bath with shower; non-working fireplace; telephone; cable television; terrycloth robes; and hair dryer.

The Sisters' Boudoir: queen bed; private bath with clawfoot tub and shower; non-working fireplace; telephone; cable television; terrycloth robes; and hair dryer.

Lucy's Garden Retreat: queen bed; private bath with whirlpool tub for two; non-working fireplace; telephone; cable television; terrycloth robes; and hair dryer.

Room rates: per night; based on single or double occupancy; corporate, military, and AAA discounts available; includes evening dessert/beverages; three-course, country gourmet breakfast. Guests' particular dietary needs accommodated whenever possible.

Late 1998 - 1999: $89 - $129

No pets permitted.
Smoking permitted only outdoors.
Children over age 12 are welcome.
Reservations encouraged.

Member: South Carolina Bed & Breakfast Association
              (SCBBA)-Charter Member
              Professional Association of Innkeepers International (PAII)
              Cooking & Baking Association of PAII

Rating: Inspected by SCBBA

MIDWEST

Michigan

Big Bay
— Big Bay Point Lighthouse Bed & Breakfast, 70-73
South Haven
— A Country Place Bed and Breakfast and Cottages, 74-78
Vassar
— The North House, 80-83

Minnesota

Wabasha
— The Anderson House, 84-89

Big Bay Point Lighthouse
Bed & Breakfast

"Anyone yearning to experience the deep solitude and unspoiled beauty of nature will find inspiration and safe haven at the inn."

— Linda and Jeff Gamble, Hosts

 **Max**, a domestic shorthair, was the irresistible "Pet of the Week" in the local paper when Linda and Jeff Gamble lived in a Chicago suburb, prior to relocating to Big Bay and becoming the proprietors of the Big Bay Point Lighthouse Bed & Breakfast. The shelter found Max on Maxwell Street, hence his name.

As a companion for Max, **Sidney** joined the family in 1996. The Gambles couldn't resist this domestic shorthair at their local pet shop, although their plans for the evening they brought Sidney home had been quite different.

"Father's Day 1996 I took Jeff out for a movie and dinner," Linda recalled. "We had some extra time after the matinee, so we went to the mall coffee shop. I decided to stop in the pet store next to the coffee shop to buy a toy for Max."

"While I was looking at fuzzy mice and balls, Jeff spotted 'Sidney' and decided he would make the perfect Father's Day gift for Max. Needlesstosay, with a new, eight-week-old kitten, we never made it to dinner!" Linda said.

Max and Sidney have become best friends, and both cats spend most of their time in the proprietors' apartment where they love to "stalk" two footstools designed in the shape of bears.

"Max and Sidney love to 'stalk our bears' until someone makes one of them move," said Linda. "Then, the two brave hunters run for their lives and hide!"

While sleeping is among Max's favorite things to do, Sidney enjoys chasing imaginary things around the Gamble's home. They both enjoy the attention of guests, and visit the inn when invited. They are not allowed to roam the b & b at will, nor do they venture outside.

Ninety years after being built to guide mariners along the remote and rocky stretch of coastline along Lake Superior, the Big Bay Point Lighthouse was converted into a bed & breakfast in 1986. One of the few surviving resident lighthouses in the country, the Big Bay Point Lighthouse sits high atop a cliff that juts into this great lake, affording guests an unparalleled view of the majestic Huron Mountains, brilliant night sky, as well as the ever-changing face of the lake, grasses and pine forest below.

In the quaint hamlet of Big Bay, only three miles away, guests will find a sandy beach, boat and bicycle rentals, tennis courts, wilderness/waterfall

Sidney & Max

tours, three gift shops, and restaurants. Museums, antique shops, and winter sports, including cross-country skiing, downhill skiing, and snowmobiling, can be found nearby. And the Pictured Rocks National Lakeshore is approximately a 90-minute drive.

For those who'd rather remain around the b & b, don't miss the opportunity to take a guided lighthouse tour, which are conducted Tuesdays, Thursdays and Sundays at 1 p.m. and 2 p.m. (Eastern Time), May through September. Admission is two dollars. The grounds of the lighthouse are open daily from 10 a.m. to 4 p.m. (Eastern Time).

Avid preservationists who were once actively-involved in the restoration of the Frank Lloyd Wright Home and Studio in Oak Park, Illinois, Linda and Jeff have committed to the historic preservation of this working lighthouse since taking up residence in 1992. The adaptive use of this lighthouse as an inn secures its long-term survival.

The inn's grounds also offer virtually unlimited opportunities for walks and hikes among the three acres of lawns, 40 acres of woods, nature trails and half-mile of lakefront property. Afterwards, relax in the sauna in the light tower or in front of the living room fireplace.

"Anyone yearning to experience the deep solitude and unspoiled beauty of nature will find inspiration and safe haven at the Big Bay Point Lighthouse Bed & Breakfast," said Linda and Jeff.

The inn is listed in the National Register of Historic Places.

Big Bay Point Lighthouse
Bed & Breakfast

PHOTO BY ANN GOLDEN

3 Lighthouse Road
Big Bay, Michigan 49808
Telephone: 906-345-9957
FAX: 906-345-9418
E-Mail: Keepers@LighthouseBandB.Com
Web Site: www.lighthousebandb.com

Proprietors/Hosts:
Linda and Jeff Gamble

30 miles/45 minutes from Marquette, Michigan
477 miles/9 hours from Detroit

Guestrooms: (7): each with private bath; no in-room telephones or televisions.

(2) *Keepers Rooms:* large room; queen bed; private bath; fireplace; lake view.

(1) *Keepers Room:* large room; queen bed; private bath with whirlpool tub; fireplace; lake view.

Assistants Rooms: queen bed; private bath; lake view.

Helpers Rooms: double bed; private bath; woods view.

Room rates: per night; includes full country breakfast served family-style; a portion of the room rate is used to support the preservation and continued restoration of the lighthouse.

	May 1 - Oct. 31	Nov. 1 - April 30
Keepers Rooms	$175	$145
Assistants Rooms	$135	$105
Helpers Rooms	$115	$85

No pets permitted.
Smoking permitted only outside.
Children age 16 and older are welcome.

Member: Michigan Lake to Lake Bed & Breakfast
              Professional Association of Innkeepers International

A Country Place
Bed and Breakfast and Cottages

"This is our home and we treat our guests on a very personal level. Of all the bed & breakfasts in our area, ours is truly considered a traditional one. This is our thirteenth year of being in business and our return business accounts for about 80 percent of our business."

— **Lee and Art Niffenegger, Hosts**

 Lee and Art Niffenegger adopted **Munchkin** from a local shelter when she was just four-weeks-old and weighed only one pound, hoping that bringing her into their home would help fill the hole in their heart having lost their previous cat. Today, this 13-pound "munchkin," who also answers to Munchie, insists on being the first to greet guests.

"She hears the doorbell and never misses greeting our guests with us," Lee said.

The gray-and-white domestic shorthair walks ahead of guests so when they reach the carpeting in the common area, she'll roll over on her back, ready for a tummy and chin rub.

"This is her way of saying 'hello,'" Art added. "This ritual is usually enjoyed by all participants. It is always enjoyed by Munchie."

As her name implies, Munchie also enjoys eating, curling up in the kitchen chair, or laying in the sun. Although she's allowed outside (she usually goes out one door and comes in another), she is primarily an indoor kitty. She's not supposed to be in the guestrooms, but it's difficult for her to resist when the invitation is extended.

And whenever guests write comments about their stay, it's Munchie that gets mentioned.

"Munchie is mentioned many times throughout our guest-book and in the numerous thank-you cards we receive," Art said. "She is loved by us and everyone who loves a cat."

The same can be said about **Miss Patience**. This offspring of a stray that lived in the Niffeneggers' woods made her presence known one day. As soon as Art and Lee discovered that the kitten had an injured eye, they made it their mission to get her the medical attention

Munchkin

she needed. Lee recalled how she spent many a hour for nearly four months trying to win the kitty's trust.

"She tore at my heartstrings, especially when she would roll over and purr when she was five feet from me, never allowing me to get closer. Her body language was saying 'pet me' and, somehow, I just had to," Lee said. "After sitting for hours next to her food pan and

coaxing her to come near, she always managed to have more patience than I did. Hence the name, Miss Patience."

But Lee's persistence paid off. With a little help from a tranquilizer, she was able to catch Miss Patience by her tail. After medical help and lots of TLC, she was saved. Although her eye couldn't be saved, she manages beautifully with the other one.

Because of Miss Patience's previous out-of-doors experience, she never goes outside. Miss P or Sweet P, as she's also known, never goes in the guestrooms, either, as she is afraid of most people. Some guests may get a glimpse of this tuxedo cat in the family room, and a few may even get to touch her.

She loves to romp with her toy mice and play fight with Munchie, who loves her, despite the fact that Miss Patience insists she's boss.

A Country Place Bed and Breakfast and Cottages is situated on five acres of woodland with a beach access to Lake Michigan one-half block away, the ideal setting for a restful and romantic getaway. Guests appreciate lazy days sunning themselves on the spacious deck, reading a book or birdwatching in the screened-in gazebo, or being entertained by the "resident wild turkeys," all the while helping themselves to the complimentary refreshing beverages and freshly-baked goodies.

Miss Patience

But if guests prefer more activity, nearby there's fishing (perch and salmon charter fishing boats available); golfing (three courses within seven miles); hiking and biking (along the 34-mile Kal-Haven Trail State Park to Kalamazoo); wine tours and tastings (two wineries within 20 minutes); walking; tennis; and shopping. Jet ski rentals and parasailing are available at the South Haven Harbor, which also allows mooring and launching of personal watercraft. For sailors and non-sailors alike,

the Michigan Maritime Museum offers a wealth of Great Lakes History.

A visit to South Haven wouldn't be complete without walking along the beautiful sandy shores of Lake Michigan.

Many fruits and vegetables, including blueberries and peaches, are grown in the South Haven-area. Lee and Art can direct guests to the many U-Pick orchards and farms. And don't forget to ask the Niffeneggers about one of their favorite local spots.

"Sherman Dairy offers some of the best homemade ice cream with the most generous portions one will find anywhere," they concurred.

79 North Shore Drive N.
South Haven, Michigan 49090
Telephone: 616-637-5523
FAX: 616-639-1998
E-Mail: acountryplace@cybersol.com
Web Site:
www.csi-net.net/acountryplace

Proprietors/Hosts:
Lee and Art Niffenegger

120 miles/2 hours from Chicago
180 miles/3 hours from Detroit

Guestrooms: (5)
Terrace Room: queen bed; private bath with shower;
$75 per night.

Meadow Room: queen bed; private bath with shower;
$85 per night.

Vineyard Room: queen bed; private bath with tub and shower, antique water closet and pedestal sink; $90 per night.

Garden Room: queen and double bed; private bath with shower; $90 per night.

Windsor Room: king bed; private bath with jet tub and shower; television; $110 per night.

Cottages: (3)
Fern Glen Cottage: sleeps 2 - 4 (dual king bed on main floor; small loft with two twin beds); great room; free-standing wood-burning fireplace; air conditioning; porches; fully-equipped kitchen with microwave; cable television; charcoal grill; located on b & b premises; uses beach access one-half block away. $500, summer weekly rate; $85 per night, spring and fall.

The Belvedere: sleeps 4 - 6 (two queen beds and bunk beds); porch; fully-equipped kitchen with microwave; cable television; charcoal grill; located on Lake Michigan; private beach; $800, summer weekly rate; $120 per night, spring and fall.

The Retreat: sleeps 2 - 4 (queen and double bed); gas fireplace; air conditioning in bedroom; ceiling fans; porch; fully-equipped kitchen with microwave; cable television; charcoal grill; located on Lake Michigan; private beach; $750, summer weekly rate; $115 per night, spring and fall.

Room rates: per night; based on double occupancy; includes "sin"sational full breakfast served fireside in the formal dining room, on the enclosed porch, in the screened-in gazebo, or on the spacious outside deck; ample parking for cars and boats.

Rooms	$75 - $110

Cottage rates: do not include breakfast; ample parking for cars and boats; children welcome; porta-cribs available.

	Per Night Spring & Fall	Weekly Summer
Cottages	$85 - $120	$500 - $800

No pets permitted.
Smoking permitted only outside.
Open April 1 to November 1 only.

Member: Michigan Lake to Lake Bed and Breakfast
              Association
              The Lakeshore Convention and Visitors Bureau
              Local Chamber of Commerce

Rating: Inspected by Michigan Lake to Lake Bed and
              Breakfast Association

The North House

"Step back in time with your hosts, who are true believers in the calmer, saner pace of yesteryear."

—Pat Akers-Goggans and Roger Goggans, Hosts

Harley Davidson, a domestic shorthair with obvious Maine Coon heritage, was named by Pat and Roger Goggans' son because she was the only Harley he could afford.

The Goggans' son had found her meowing while walking at a local wildlife refuge. She obviously had been abandoned along with her kittens, and he spent all the money he had to buy food and try to make them comfortable. The following day, when Pat learned what her son had done, she sent him back to the wildlife refuge to rescue them, but this time he could only find the mother cat. He brought her home, alerting the local authorities and calling back every day to see if someone had found the kittens, but

that never happened. It took a while for Harley to mellow since at the beginning she associated the Goggans with the loss of her family.

It took another few years for her to warm up to guests, but along with the affection came a knack for discerning cat lovers from those who aren't feline fans.

"We have no idea how she knows, but she's never failed to be accurate," Pat said.

With her earlier exposure to the outdoors, Harley remains an indoor/outdoor cat. She still enjoys the challenge of a good hunt, but has discovered that a cat fishing pole or ball can be exciting as well. If invited, she'll join guests in their rooms.

Harley Davidson

Pat said she wouldn't be surprised if Black Beauty surpasses the pup size-wise.

"He has enormous feet so we predict he will become a very large gentleman and regal master of all he surveys," Pat said.

This 1880 Victorian home built for Townsend North, the founder of Vassar, Michigan, has been preserved and transformed into a bed & breakfast by Pat and Roger.

After nearly 19 years together, the Goggans were separated from their senior cat, Tater. Shortly after, Pat found a black kitten crying under a parked car across the street from The North House. She said the shape of his head and body indicates he has Siamese somewhere in him, and she expects him to grow into a true beauty, hence the name **Black Beauty**.

He's taking his direction from Harley, joining guests in their rooms when the invitation is extended as well as playing with the kitty fishing pole. He's also making it known that he can hold his own with another new member of the family, the Goggans' puppy who is supposed to be full-grown at six pounds.

Since the Goggans believe in the calmer pace of yesteryear, the five guestrooms and one suite have neither televisions nor telephones. Adding to the solitude is the acre of groomed

Black Beauty

lawn and shady glade for quiet strolls, private picnics, or reading. If you didn't bring along a book, the Goggans invite you to borrow one from their library.

After the full, four-course breakfast, guests are invited to take a tour of the house, which counts Samuel Clemons and Thomas Edison among its most noted visitors. This house is listed in the National Register of Historic Places.

Guests also can take advantage of nearby tennis, golf, horseback riding, year-round ice skating, cross-country skiing, and shopping, including the 200-store outlet mall 20 minutes away. Fishing or canoeing on the Cass River, conveniently-located a few blocks away, also will help restore, refresh, and revive, according to the Goggans.

Vassar also is an hour's drive from the shores of Lake Huron.

The North House

325 N. Main St.
Vassar, Michigan 48768-1322
Telephone: 517-823-3047
FAX: 517-752-9188
E-Mail: rgoggans@aol.com
Web Site: --
Proprietors/Hosts:
Pat Akers-Goggans and Roger Goggans

95 miles/1-1/2 hours from Detroit-area
198 miles/4 hours from Mackinac Island

Guestrooms: (5): no in-room television, telephone, or air conditioning; rooms have ceiling fan and 10-foot ceilings.

(1) Suite: no in-room television, telephone, or air conditioning; suite has pedestal fan and 12-foot ceiling.

Twin Bed: shared bath; $30 per night; $125, 5-day weekly (Sunday to Thursday).

Double Bed: shared bath; $40 per night; $165, 5-day weekly (Sunday to Thursday).

Double Bed: shared bath; sitting room; $45 per night; $180, 5-day weekly (Sunday to Thursday).

Two Adjoining Rooms with Double Beds: shared bath; $75 per night; $300, 5-day weekly (Sunday to Thursday).

North Family Master Suite: king canopy bed; private bath; $65 per night; $275, 5-day weekly (Sunday to Thursday); with adjacent private living room, $85 per night; $350, 5-day weekly (Sunday to Thursday).

Room/suite rates: includes full, four-course breakfast featuring home-grown, home-preserved (or fresh in season) fruits, jams, and jellies; breakfast served in the formal dining room or, weather-permitting, on the deck; 10 percent discount extended to clergy or church-business guests; multiple rooms also may qualify for special rates.

	Per Night	5-Day Weekly (Sunday - Thursday)
Rooms	$30 - $75	$125 - $300
North Family Master Suite	$65	$275
North Family Master Suite with Living Room	$85	$350

Pet-friendly.
Smoking permitted only on first-floor porch and second-floor porch.

The Anderson House

"Come experience country inn tradition at The Anderson House. Virtually nothing has changed since Grandma Anderson left a heritage of caring and sharing. Her priorities, service, comfort, great interest, and excellent food are as important now as then."

— John S. Hall, Host

R.B. or **Arby** is the senior statesman of The Anderson House's 11 cats. He found a home at the historic hotel after he was found living outside by a couple in Rochester, Minnesota. He is somewhat shy, definitely doesn't like to be held, and since the time that five-year-old twin girls dressed him in baby clothes, he's no longer fond of kids. But this domestic shorthair does love his treats.

Arnold also is on the shy side and shies away from children. He came to The Anderson House from a local animal shelter, a gift from an author who made a book presentation at the hotel. Arnold was named for the cat in the book. This domestic shorthair loves to eat and be brushed, but not necessarily in that order.

Arnold

R.B.

Buttons, another domestic shorthair, is a favorite with a couple who now comes annually just to spend time with him.

Buttons

they were just six-months-old, they are accustomed to guests and are quite friendly. Tiger's put on a few pounds since then, while Fred has been known to waddle down the hallway as well, in search of an open guestroom.

Tiger

"They now come once a year and have for the past eight years," said Elizabeth Hall. "He is such a mellow cat."

Buttons was brought to the hotel by a family when he was just a kitten. When he's not sleeping — his favorite way to pass the time — he can be guest-friendly, but he does have his shy moments.

Fred, and his brother **Tiger**, both domestic shorthairs, can

Fred

best be described as "big babies" and love to be treated as such. Having come to The Anderson House from a family in Winona, Minnesota when

"Tiger is one of the biggest and fattest cats at The Anderson House," Elizabeth said. "It just goes to show how well they are fed."

When a couple moved to a retirement home and couldn't take **Ginger** with them, she came to live at The Anderson House. This domestic shorthair is so friendly she'll jump on a guest's shoulder to greet them when they come into the "cats' room," the felines' private sanctuary.

Goblin was one of two kittens born to a cat that decided to

Ginger

Max, a tabby cat, and his brother, **Midnight**, a black domestic longhair, came from a Minneapolis family who wanted them to remain in the same household. Max is a lot like Fred and Tiger in that he loves to be

Mickey

give birth underneath the kitchen crawl space. This domestic longhair doesn't seem to have a shy bone in his body. He loves to play and he loves people.

Although **Mickey** is one of the younger cats, she has assumed a position of leadership. This domestic longhair took to a new toy that none of the other cats had shown any interest in. But once she started to play with it,

Goblin

the other cats followed. Although she has bouts of shyness, Mickey is generally quite friendly.

craddled like a baby. He can be friendly, but has his share of shy moments. Midnight's friendlier and more playful. He loves to grab the faucet drain plug with his front paws and pull it out. If Elizabeth puts it back, he'll pull it out again. Since he

Max

Midnight

plays hard, he also enjoys his downtime.

The youngest of The Anderson House cats, **Bambie**, found her way to the Hall's residence and meowed so loudly that John couldn't ignore her. The Hall family kept her for two months before bringing her to the hotel. Except for her reluctance to being held, this Calico is friendly, loves to play, and seems to have adjusted quite well to life with 10 other cats and the countless cat-loving guests who call The Anderson House home away from home.

Located in a residential section of Wabasha, The Anderson House is the oldest, continuously operating hotel in Minnesota, having first opened its doors in 1856.

According to John, the hotel's warmth and cheer is reminiscent of a bygone era.

"There is a feeling of time having stopped as you wonder through the antique-filled rooms with their high beds, marble-topped dressers, handmade quilts, Victorian pictures, paintings and framed marriage certificates," John said.

The Anderson House has been in the Hall family since 1896, and John is the fourth generation to own and operate the 25-room hotel. The ever-filled cookie jar at the front desk is just one example of Grandma Anderson's personality and plans that continue to be felt.

Bambie

"Virtually nothing has changed since Grandma Anderson left a heritage of caring and sharing. Her priorities, service, comfort, great interest, and excellent food are as important now as then," John said.

Authored by John and Jeanne Hall, the fourth and largest of The Anderson House cookbooks was published in 1986. Recipes for many of the items featured on Anderson House menus can be found in the cookbook, which specializes in Dutch Oven home cooking.

Another tradition that sets The Anderson House apart is the resident cats, which have been a special part since 1976.

Repeat guests can inquire at the time they make their reservation if their favorite feline is available to join them in their guestroom during their stay. The hotel provides a cat bed, food, and water so that the cats don't stray from their regular diet. For first-time guests who want a cat to stay with them, only if the kitty to whom they've

a taken a liking reciprocates those feelings will they spend time together.

For those who prefer non-feline accommodations, guestrooms nos. 2, 15, and 34 are off-limits to the cats.

Wabasha, one of the last of the Old Rivertowns, is a stopping point for two riverboats. The Mississippi River, lake and sloughs provide a wide variety of options for fishing. The Hiawatha Valley area also offers golf, bicycling, tennis, eagle watching, downhill and cross-country skiing, snowmobiling, and shopping at the Antique Center and Factory Outlet Gift Shop.

The Anderson House is listed in the National Register of Historic Places.

The Anderson House

333 Main Street West
Wabasha, Minnesota 55981
Telephone: 612-565-4524
Toll-free Reservations: 1-800-535-5467
FAX: 612-565-4003
E-Mail: andtours@wabasha.net
Web Site: www.theandersonhouse.com

Proprietors/Hosts:
John, John, Jr., Joseph,
and Elizabeth Hall

85 miles/1-1/2 hours from Minneapolis
40 miles/45 minutes from Rochester, Minnesota

Guestrooms: (25); (22) with private bath; (3) with shared baths.
(5) suites, including three with whirlpool tubs.

Mayo Suite: built for Will and Charlie Mayo of the Mayo Clinic
who would spend weekends at The Anderson House when their
yacht was moored in Wabasha.

Lincoln Suite: named because the furniture dates back to this
period in history; President Harry S. Truman and First Lady
Bess Truman stayed in this suite during one of his many train
trips.

Bridal Suite: popular with honeymooners; oversized bed and
whirlpool tub.

Room/suite rates: per night; September and October rates slightly higher.

	1998	1999
Room with shared bath	$50	$55
Room with private bath	$69 - $99	$69 - $109
Suite	$100 - $129	$105 - $139
Whirlpool Suite	$115 - $139	$119 - $149

Packages available that include dinner and breakfast; breakfast delivered to guestroom upon request.

Pet-friendly.
Smoking permitted only in designated guestrooms. Restaurant
is non-smoking.
Open continuously April 1 - November 1; winter hours apply
November 1 - March 31.

NORTHWEST

Idaho
Sandpoint
— The Coit House Bed & Breakfast, 92-94

Oregon
Newport
— The Sylvia Beach Hotel, 96-99

The Coit House
Bed & Breakfast

"Walk through our doors and experience the magnificent beauty of a restored 1907 Victorian manor."

— Julie and Seth Coit, Hosts

To show their appreciation for business, realtors certainly have sent flowers or plants to their clients. But the real estate agent who sold Julie and Seth Coit the Victorian house that they remodeled and transformed into The Coit House Bed & Breakfast presented them with a different gift entirely.

"Tom and **Jerry** were given to us during the remodeling process because we thought we had a rodent problem," Julie recalled. "The alleged problem definitely was solved once the cats 'cleaned house.'"

Although these domestic long-hairs are brothers, they have very different personalities.

"Tommy is very dominant and regal," Julie said. "He rolls over from side-to-side when he greets guests but is quite selective about whom he befriends."

Jerry, on the other hand, tends to sit back and observe.

Apparently, a greater force felt that The Coit House was meant to have three cats. Also during the remodeling process, Julie made her daily trek to the county dump. But one day she varied her routine slightly.

"Usually, I simply stopped at the attendant station, then proceeded to the area where I was instructed to unload the truck. As a fluke, this very cold January day I got out of the truck and from out of nowhere, a tiny kitten ran to me and literally jumped into my arms," Julie said.

Even though she already had Tom and Jerry, Julie knew she could not leave him behind.

"The vet said he probably would not have made it another day," Julie said.

They named him **Dollar** — poetic justice for the well-spent dollars incurred nursing him back to health. A domestic shorthair, Dollar also is known as Dolly.

All three cats enjoy sunbathing by day. In the evening, they eagerly-await their treats, rubs, and brushings. Julie admits that they are "her" boys.

Both Julie and Seth are insistent that neither Dollar, Tom, or Jerry, nor their three dogs set a paw in the guestrooms.

While they are animal lovers, they respect that not all their guests share their feelings and even those who do may have allergies.

 This 1907 Victorian manor has been meticulously restored and furnished with antiques by Julie and Seth, renaming it The Coit House when they opened its doors as a b & b in 1995.

Just blocks from downtown Sandpoint with its shops, restaurants, and city beach, the b & b also is conveniently-located near Lake Pend Oreille for fishing, Schweitzer Mountain Resort for downhill and cross-country skiing, as well as tennis, golf, horseback riding, and walking/hiking/biking paths.

Tommy, Jerry & Dollar

The Coit House
Bed & Breakfast

502 North Fourth Avenue
Sandpoint, Idaho 83864
Telephone: 208-265-4035
FAX: 208-265-4035
E-Mail: --
Web Site:
www.keokee.com/lodgecenresv
Proprietors/Hosts:
Julie and Seth Coit

79 miles/1-1/2 hours from Spokane, Washington
179 miles/3-1/2 hours from Kalispell, Montana
321 miles/6 hours from Banff, British Columbia, Canada

Guestrooms: (2): each with private bath; cable television; telephone.
(2) suites: each with private bath; cable television; telephone.

Room A (Upstairs Master Suite): sleigh bed; private bath with clawfoot tub.
Room B: ornate brass bed; private bath; one-of-a-kind antiques.
Room C: intricate wooden poster bed; private bath; one-of-a-kind antiques.
Room D (Downstairs Master Suite): handcrafted column bed; private bath with clawfoot tub.

Room/suite rates: per night; includes full breakfast with fresh-baked breads and pastries.

| | Winter | | Summer | |
	Single	Double	Single	Double
Rooms & Suites	$55 - $65	$65 - $75	$75	$85 - $90

No pets permitted.
Smoking permitted only outside.
Children over age 12 are welcome.

Rating: AAA Three Diamond Award (1998)

The Silvia Beach Hotel

"Sylvia Beach Hotel is an eclectic, comfortable place to let go of the stresses of daily routine, to relax and read, write and converse face-to-face, and to enjoy the company of like-minded people."

— ***Charlotte Dinolt and Ken Peyton, Hosts***

Since the hotel owners and staff at the Sylvia Beach Hotel are all cat lovers, they knew that sooner or later there would be another cat to love since Jersey, the resident cat since Halloween Eve 1991, was no longer with them. It just happened sooner than later.

Stella New Jersey was discovered on the doorstep of a Portland, Oregon home, about a two-and-a-half hour drive from the hotel, with a note that simply stated her family couldn't keep her. As luck would have it, this family had been preparing to welcome another kitten into their home, so they called the Sylvia Beach to see how they felt about adopting a 13-week-old kitten (who at the time was known as Lily).

Hotel Manager Charlotte Dinolt said they were thrilled with the call, and the Portland family was so appreciative that they drove Stella to her new home — none too soon since she hadn't taken too kindly to the other kittten.

Charlotte explained that Stella was named for the heroine in *A Streetcar Named Desire* by Tennessee Williams, one of the well-known authors for which the hotel's guestrooms are named. And since this black kitty with white markings bears a strong resemblance to Jersey, her full name became Stella New Jersey.

Unlike her reaction to the kitten, Stella immediately took to

Stella New Jersey

lovers in mind. Each of the 20 guestrooms is named and decorated for a well-known author. The ocean-front library ascends into the attic where guests also will find a cozy fireplace. Current titles are available in the hotel's gift shop. Even the hotel restaurant carries on the literary theme. Tables of Content, which faces the ocean, offers one seating for dinner during the week and two on the weekends. The award-winning cuisine is served family style. Reservations are required. Smoking is not permitted. The restaurant also is where guests enjoy breakfast each morning from 8:30 a.m. to 10 a.m.

her new family, ingratiating herself with the staff and guests alike. Within a week, she carried on Jersey's legacy of spending the night with those who want the company, welcome news for the hotel's cat-loving guests.

"She was meant to be here," Charlotte added.

Located on NW Cliff Street overlooking the surf at Nye Beach, this hotel was built between 1910 and 1912. Originally named the New Cliff House, it operated for a time as the Hotel Gilmore. As a tribute to Sylvia Beach, one of the century's greatest patrons of literature, the hotel was renamed in 1987 by new owners Sally Ford and Goody Cable.

The Sylvia Beach is unique in that it's designed with book

In addition to reading and exploring new worlds vicariously, guests at the Sylvia Beach enjoy the beach — purr-fect for daydreaming or walking. There's also hiking, tennis, golf, biking, horseback riding, fishing, and shopping. Popular spots in the area include the Oregon Coast Aquarium or Hatfield Marine Sciences Center, Cascade Head, Cape Perpetua, and the Sand Dunes.

The hotel has been listed in the National Register of Historic Places since 1986.

The Sylvia Beach Hotel

267 NW Cliff Street
Newport, Oregon 97365
Telephone: 541-265-5428
FAX: --
E-Mail: --
Web Site: --

Proprietors/Hosts:
Sally Ford and Goody Cable
Managers/Hosts:
Charlotte Dinolt and Ken Peyton

122 miles/2-1/2 hours from Portland, Oregon
110 miles/2-1/4 hours from Eugene, Oregon

Guestrooms: (20): each with private bath; no in-room telephones, radios, or televisions.

Classic:

Agatha Christie: queen bed; trundle/hide-a-bed; private bath; fireplace; deck; oceanfront/west view.

Mark Twain: queen bed; private bath; fireplace; deck; oceanfront/west view.

Colette: queen bed; two single beds; private bath; fireplace; deck; oceanfront/west view.

Best Sellers:

Herman Melville: king bed; private bath; ocean/north view.

Sigrid Undset, Hemingway, Tennessee Williams, Emily Dickinson, and F. Scott Fitzgerald: queen bed; private bath; ocean/north view.

Meridel Le Sueur: queen bed; trundle/twin bed; private bath; ocean/south view.

Alice Walker, Lincoln Steffens, Jane Austen, and Edgar Allan Poe: double bed; private bath; ocean/north view.

E.B. White: twin beds; private bath; ocean/north view.

Dr. Seuss: twin beds; private bath; deck; north view.

Novels:

R.L. Stevenson: queen bed; private bath; deck; garden/south view.

Willa Cather: double bed; private bath; deck; garden/south view.

Gertrude Stein: double bed; private bath; south view.

Oscar Wilde: twin beds; private bath; south view.

Room rates: per night; based on double occupancy; $10 less for single occupancy; $15 extra for third person in room; includes full breakfast; complimentary hot wine served nightly in the library.

	10/25/98 - 12/10/98 Weekends & Holidays	Weekdays	12/11/98 - 1/2/99	1/3/99 - Weekends & Holidays	3/11/99 Weekdays
CLASSIC	$152	$152	$152	$152	$152
BEST SELLERS	$103	$89	$103	$103	$89
NOVELS	$69	$63	$69	$69	$63

	3/12/99 - 4/10/99	4/11/99 - Weekends & Holidays	5/13/99 Weekdays
CLASSIC	$152	$152	$152
BEST SELLERS	$103	$103	$89
NOVELS	$69	$69	$63

Restaurant available for private group functions.

No pets permitted.
Smoking permitted only outdoors.
Hotel not suitable for small children.

WEST

California
Dulzura
— Brookside Farm Bed and Breakfast Inn, 102-106
Laguna Beach
— Casa Laguna Bed & Breakfast Inn, 108-110
San Francisco
— Golden Gate Hotel, 112-115
— The Sherman House, 116-119

Colorado
Colorado Springs
— AwareNest Victorian Bed & Breakfast, 120-122
— Holden House - 1902 Bed and Breakfast Inn, 124-128
— The Painted Lady Bed & Breakfast Inn, 130-133
Loveland
— Wild Lane Bed & Breakfast Inn, 134-137
Redstone
— Crystal Dreams Bed & Breakfast, 138-140

Oklahoma
Oklahoma City
– The Grandison at Maney Park, 142-145

Brookside Farm
Bed and Breakfast Inn

Adrienne, named for Adrienne "A.J." Gustin, a cat-loving guest, was the first resident cat at Brookside Farm Bed and Breakfast Inn. The mixed tiger was an adopted stray with an incredibly caring nature. While nursing her own kittens, she adopted and nurtured an abandoned litter. She has since turned her attention and affection to guests. Seemingly shy at first, if she takes a liking to a guest, she'll curl up and sleep on their lap for hours. Adrienne will even follow a guest to their room, walking a bit stiffly because of the arthritis in her back legs. But at age 10, she's entitled to take her time.

Not necessarily looking to adopt another cat, the Guishards dis-

covered **Talia's** picture on the bulletin board at the post office. They couldn't resist this beautiful Norwegian Forest cat, so they took her home, keeping the name her original owner had given her. She's quite the "conversationalist" and loves to be petted, but doesn't take to being picked up. She, too, is allowed in the guestrooms.

Francis, a big mixed breed that bears a resemblance to a Maine Coon, was named for another guest, Frances Tapscott. When they selected the name, the Guishards thought he was a she, because they found "her" at an old trailer along with two black-and-white kitties and presumed "she" was the mother cat. Sally and Edd made sure the kittens found caring homes as well.

"We gave the kittens away to guests but *had* to keep Francis

Adrienne

as they arrive. He's the official greeter, and even walks guests to their room, where he'll stay if invited.

as he is the most loving cat imaginable," Sally said. "Shortly after we brought him home, the vet pointed out that Francis was a male."

Sally said fate brought them all together.

"Weeks before his family abandoned him, we heard him up in a neighbor's tree crying and crying. I made our handyman climb a ladder and get him down," Sally said. "He was destined to be our Francis."

The youngest of the Guishard's cats is **Nellie**, a Calico, who was the pick of the litter in Sally's eyes. Nellie was named after a heroine in an English novel.

Talia

Francis likes to perch atop the desk to see the guests

Francis

"Our friends had a litter of Calicos and I picked her out when she was only one-week-old," Sally said.

However, once they brought her home, they discovered she's not fond of other cats. She also remains aloof around the guests, preferring to "look beautiful" and sleep, especially in

Captain Small's Room, one of the guestrooms in the farm-house.

Refurbished by Sally and Edd as a bed and break-fast in 1983, this 1928 farmhouse and barrel-roofed stone barn is true to its name. The ever-changing livestock population currently includes Pricilla, the pig; Prince and Tangie, the goats; Elvis, the pheasant; as well as chickens and geese galore. Aviaries house parakeets, doves, quail, and peacocks.

The vegetable gardens and fruit trees provide much of the ingre-dients for Edd's culinary mas-terpieces, which he showcases daily at breakfast, the light weekday suppers, and the optional weekend gourmet din-ners, where guests may help prepare the meal in exchange for recipes and cooking tips.

The bed and breakfast creates a restful oasis, especially with the addition of the secluded hot tub, the purr-fect spot for star-gaz-ing or a natural follow-up to a massage, available only on Saturdays.

Nellie

For those who desire more activity or want to try and burn off a few calories after savoring Edd's creations, there's bicy-cling, golf, horseback riding, walking/hiking, even horse-shoes.

San Diego, El Cajon, and Tecate, Mexico also are nearby. If guests want to explore the local history, there's the South-western Railroad Museum and rides in Campo; the empty mines from Dulzura's "under-whelming" gold rush of 1908; and relics of the area's early inhabitants, the San Dieguito Indians.

Brookside Farm
Bed and Breakfast Inn

1373 Marron Valley Road
Dulzura, California 91914
Telephone: 619-468-3043
FAX: 619-468-9145
E-Mail: --
Web Site: --

Proprietors/Hosts:
Sally and Edd Guishard

30 miles/40 minutes from San Diego

Guestrooms: (7) rooms: no in-room telephone or television.
(3) suites: no in-room telephone or television.

Farmhouse Rooms and Cottage:
Sun Porch: queen bed; private bath with shower; outside
entrance through a private patio; $80 per night; $220 gourmet
weekend rate.

Wine Cellar: four-poster queen bed; private bath with shower;
outside entrance; $80 per night; $220 gourmet weekend rate.

Captain Small's Room: queen bed; private bath with clawfoot
tub; private screened porch; $80 per night; $220 gourmet
weekend rate.

Oak View Room: queen bed; private bath; outside entrance;
$80 per night; $220 gourmet weekend rate.

New Rose Room: queen bed; private bath with tub and shower;
fireplace; private balcony; refrigerator; coffee service; $105 per
night; $270 gourmet weekend rate.

Hunter's Cabin: queen bed; private bath with tub and shower;
wood-burning stove; refrigerator; $95 per night; $250 gourmet
weekend rate.

Stone Barn Rooms:
Room With A View: queen bed; private bath; private balcony
with panoramic view of back-country mountains; see-through
fireplace; refrigerator; coffee service; $115 per night; $290
gourmet weekend rate.

Jennie's Room: queen bed; Victorian hideaway on top floor;
elegant bathroom with shower; separate tub by fireplace; refrigerator; coffee service; $115 per night; $290 gourmet weekend
rate.

Peter Rabbit's House: queen bed, plus day bed; private bath with tub/shower; large screened porch; wood-burning stove; refrigerator; $85 per night; $230 weekend rate.

La Casita: queen bed; private bath with oversized tub and shower; gas-log fireplace; private courtyard; $85 per night; $230 gourmet weekend rate.

Room/suite rates: based on double occupancy; includes full country breakfast; complimentary light supper at 6:30 p.m., Monday - Thursday. Gourmet weekend rates include full country breakfast; four-course gourmet dinner at 7 p.m., Friday and Saturday; guests welcome to bring their own wine.

	Per Night	Gourmet Weekend Rate
Farmhouse Rooms and Cottage	$80 - $105	$220 - $270
Stone Barn Rooms	$85 - $115	$230 - $290

Guests' cats only are permitted.
Smoking permitted only outdoors.
Reservations encouraged.

Member: California Lodging Industry Association

Casa Laguna
Bed & Breakfast Inn

"Casa Laguna Inn is an enchanting Spanish-style bed and breakfast inn overlooking the blue Pacific that exudes an ambiance of bygone days."

— **Joan and Lee Kerr, and Louise and Ted Gould, Hosts**

Bully, who was born in Bullhead, California, came to the inn by way of a staff member. For at least the past seven years, this mixed breed has been Casa Laguna's resident cat. He is extremely guest-oriented, and loves to play with people, sit on their laps, and join them in their rooms, if invited.

"Bully roams the property, trying to find a guest who needs a companion or 'buddy' for the evening," said Joan Kerr.

When guests are relaxing or enjoying other activities, Bully will find other ways to entertain himself; he'll sit for hours staring at the birds in the large aviary located on the inn's property. The birds seem oblivious to Bully's presence.

But even when guests leave the inn, their thoughts are still of Bully. Joan shared that following the earthquakes that rocked the area a few years back, they received several calls from across-the-country inquiring about Bully's well-being.

"It was amusing that no one cared about the owners or the staff," Joan said. "They just wanted to be sure that Bully was OK."

Overlooking the Pacific Ocean, Casa Laguna invites guests to slow their pace to that of a less hurried era, like the bygone days when Laguna Beach was developing its reputation as a hideaway for Hollywood's film stars and an artists' colony. In addition to its

20 individually-decorated guest-rooms and suites, Casa Laguna offers five patio areas for relaxing, an outdoor heated pool with ocean views, as well as a Bell Tower Observation deck, the purr-fect place to catch spectacular sunsets over nearby Catalina Island.

Adding to the inn's tropical, romantic setting are over 700 colorful tiles, which convey an enchanting aura of the property.

The ocean is indeed a focal point, and two of the finest beaches in southern California are located directly across from Casa Laguna. The seaside resort town of Laguna Beach offers many boutiques and pottery shops, as well as over 100 art galleries. The internationally-renowned Pageant of the Masters and famed Festival of Arts has been a drawing card every July and August since its inaugural showing in 1932.

The area also affords world-class golf, cycling, tennis, fishing, and sightseeing.

Disneyland is just a 30-mile drive.

Bully

Casa Laguna
Bed & Breakfast Inn

2510 South Coast Highway
Laguna Beach, California 92651
Telephone: 714-494-2996
Toll-free Reservations: 1-800-233-0449
FAX: 714-494-5009
E-Mail: --
Web Site: --

Proprietors/Hosts:
Joan and Lee Kerr
Louise and Ted Gould

60 miles/65 minutes from Los Angeles
72 miles/80 minutes from San Diego

Guestrooms: (14) rooms: each features either a lovely garden vista or panoramic ocean view; each with private bath with shower; direct-dial telephones; cable television; many with refrigerators.
(6) Suites:

Suite 1: ocean view; oversized living room with two queen-sized sleeper sofas; dining area; full kitchen; private bath with shower; one bedroom; private balcony.

Suite 2: ocean view; living room with sleeper sofa; full kitchen; private bath with shower; two bedrooms; private balcony.

Suite 3: ocean view; living room with sleeper sofa; full kitchen; private bath with shower; one bedroom; private balcony.

Suite 4: secluded garden view of aviary patio and palms; living room with sleeper sofa; dining area; full kitchen; private bath with shower; one bedroom; private balcony.

Honeymoon Cottage: private ocean view deck; garden with potting shed; sitting room with fireplace; large living/dining room; full kitchen; private bath with shower for two; one bedroom.

The Mission House: ocean views; large living room; dining room; two fireplaces; full kitchen; private bath with shower; two bedrooms.

Room/suite rates: $79 to $249; includes continental-plus breakfast; afternoon tea; wine and hors d'oeuvres.

Small, well-mannered dogs allowed on a limited basis.
Smoking permitted only in designated guestrooms and
    public areas.
Reservations recommended.

Rating: AAA Two Diamond Award (1998)

Golden Gate Hotel

"In 1986, we settled down to create the kind of hotel we always looked for on our travels: comfortable and charming, full of flowers, perfectly-located, and serving a great cup of coffee. With the Golden Gate Hotel, we have fulfilled our dream."

— Renate, John, and Gabriele Kenaston, Hosts

A hard-to-place feral kitten has grown up to become such an important figure at the Golden Gate Hotel that he is prominently featured on the property's literature.

Captain Nemo came to the hotel about eight years ago with the "warning" that "he bites." But the Kenaston family felt confident that he'd outgrow this alleged bad habit once he was placed in a loving environment.

Their lives had changed forever a few years earlier when, seemingly out of nowhere, a frail orange cat meandered into the hotel.

"She was the sweetest, gentlest soul, a fragile, ethereal presence," said Gabriele. "She brought out the best in us and added a warmth we didn't know we were missing."

When she left as suddenly as she had appeared, she also left a void that would never be filled, but the Kenastons decided they wanted to open their hearts to a kindred spirit.

Captain Nemo, so named because even as a kitten he had an aloof aura and imperious attitude, has grown into an 18 pound black (with white chest patch) beauty, who no longer bites the hands that feed him. He loves to chase (and eat) Pounce® treats down the hall, people-watch from the sofa, sleep on chairs, and nibble on the azaleas on the windowsills.

He's an indoor kitty, except for the time a few years ago when the innkeepers decided it would be "so cute" to immortalize his pawprints in the new concrete being laid outside.

"What we got were four bleeding adults and one very offended cat," recalled Gabriele.

Regular guests leave their doors open for Captain Nemo, who has a natural affection for cat lovers, especially those who are missing their own cat companion.

"Captain Nemo will stay with them as much as possible," Gabriele said.

And to show their appreciation, guests have given him gifts. Every Christmas, Captain Nemo receives a package of catnip grown in a guest's garden. And just last holiday season, two guests presented him with a Santa hat and scarf set. Since he was enjoying catnip at the time, he posed for a photograph without complaint. A few weeks later, the Kenastons received a framed enlargement (small poster would be a more apt description) that now hangs in the office, much to Captain Nemo's dismay!

Captain Nemo

Located in the heart of San Francisco, between Union Square and the top of fashionable Nob Hill, the Golden Gate Hotel has been described by guests as cozy, quaint, charming, and one-of-a-kind. Built as a hotel in 1913, this four-story Edwardian building is surrounded by the city's finest shops, restaurants, and theaters.

"You could walk around this part of town for days and not see or do it all," Renate said.

But for those who'd rather not navigate the hills on foot, the cable car stops at the corner and whisks guests to Fisherman's Wharf, North Beach, and countless irresistible stops along the way. Other forms of public transportation go to other popular spots, including Golden Gate Park (trails for horseback riding) and the Mission District. Bicycling, tennis, and golf are close by as well.

Renate and her husband, John, have traveled and lived all over Asia and Europe. In addition to learning several languages and speaking fluent German, French, and Spanish, they have earned an appreciation for people from all corners of the world.

"John, always ready for a cup of tea, can bring the most morose arrival to a chuckle," Renate said.

The Kenastons, who have a genuine affection for their guests, have put their personal spin on the song lyrics, *I left my heart in San Francisco.*

"Our staff delights in anticipating your needs and exceeding your expectations. We want you to leave your heart at the Golden Gate Hotel," the Kenastons said.

The hotel, with its antique and wicker furnishings, boasts the oldest working birdcage elevator in the city. The parlor fireplace is a popular gathering spot no matter what the weather. And the hallways are lined with historical photographs, a unique collection begun by a former hotel employee who has since turned his passion into a profession.

Golden Gate Hotel

775 Bush Street (between Powell and Mason)
San Francisco, California 94108
Telephone: 415-392-3702
Toll-free Reservations: 1-800-835-1118
FAX: 415-392-6202
E-Mail: --
Web Site: www.goldengatehotel.com

Proprietors/Hosts:
Renate, John, and Gabriele Kenaston

16 miles/30 minutes from San Francisco International Airport

Guestrooms: (25): each with telephones; cable television.
(14) with private bath, some with clawfoot tubs; queen or twin beds.

(9) with shared bath (three rooms share one bath); all have in-room sinks; double or twin beds.

(2) share one bath; two double beds.

"Family Set-Up:" queen bed; private bath; adjoins room with twin beds; separate bath.

Room rates: per night; includes continental breakfast served in breakfast room; can be delivered to the guestroom upon request; afternoon tea and cookies in the parlor.

Room with private bath	$99 - $109
Room with shared bath	$65 - $72
"Familly Set-Up" for three	$174
"Family Set-Up" for four	$181

Pet-friendly. (One-time charge of $10; owners also liable for all damages.)
Non-smoking property.
Reservations recommended.

Member: California Association of Bed & Breakfast Inns
Professional Association of Innkeepers International
California Hotel & Motel Association

Rating: Frommer's "Super Special Value" Award

The Sherman House

Boots was a neighbor's cat that seemed to spend more time on the hotel's property than at her own home. Over time, she adopted The Sherman House, and this former Pacific Heights mansion-turned-hotel adopted her.

"It was mutual," said Christine Berlin, hotel manager.

Boots, named because she has beautiful white socks on all four legs, is a mixed breed who fits purr-fectly with the heritage, luxury, and elegance that makes this intimate grand hotel unlike any other.

She can come and go as she pleases — outdoors in the formal gardens with its gazebo, in the lobby, upstairs sitting room,

and sometimes even in the guestrooms. One of The Sherman House's frequent celebrity guests monopolized her time during his stay.

"When Marlon Brando was staying with us, Boots stayed in his room the entire time," Christine said. "He would order roomservice for her. After he left, it was difficult to get her to go back to cat food."

But guests don't have to be movie stars to get Boots' attention or affection. Some even want to take her home (and to some very luxurious homes, too!) but all offers have been — and will continue to be — refused.

"She's extremely friendly with the guests. She's always looking for someone to pet her (or feed her)," Christine said.

Ah, the way to Boots' heart may just be through her stomach!

Built in 1876 for Leander Sherman, a great patron of music and a major force in establishing San Francisco's symphony and opera, this Victorian home became a hotel in 1983. Having served as Sherman's home for 50 years, economic times had changed such that it was no longer deemed financially-feasible to continue as a private residence. Only its designation as a San Francisco landmark and the generosity and foresight of Manou and Vesta Mobedshahi preserved and restored it for future generations to enjoy.

The grand piano in the living room/salon is reminiscent of the days when Sherman's "guests" would oblige with impromptu concerts. Now it's The Sherman House guests, amateur and professional alike, who perform. Sometimes the finches that reside in an oversized birdcage, a replica of a French chateau, sing to the accompaniment or sing a cappella.

The Sherman House features a fabulous dining room exclusively for its guests. In addition to offering breakfast, lunch, and dinner prepared by Executive Chef Tsvika Silberberg, known for his French-California creations, there is 24-hour room-service for those who prefer the intimacy of in-room dining.

The hotel encourages its guests to call upon the concierge/reservation staff to ensure their stay is everything — and more — than they expected.

Those who want to explore the Pacific Heights section of the city will find boutiques and antique shops within walking distance. The San Francisco-area also is a bonanza for those who want to bike, play tennis, golf, not to mention enjoy international shopping and world-class cuisine.

Boots

The Sherman House

2160 Green Street
San Francisco, California 94123
Telephone: 415-563-3600
FAX: 415-563-1882
E-Mail: TSHREZ@MHOTELGROUP.COM
Web Site: www.MHotelgroup.com

Proprietors/Hosts:
Manou and Vesta Mobedshahi
Manager/Host:
Christine Berlin

24 miles/30 - 45 minutes from San Francisco International Airport

Guestrooms (8): each with private bath.
(6) Suites: each with private bath, several with whirlpool tubs.

The Main House

The Lillian Russell Room (#101): half-canopy queen feather bed; private bath; wood-burning fireplace; view of Carriage House and formal gardens; $335 per night.

The Garden Room (#102): half-canopy queen feather bed; private bath; wood-burning fireplace; view of Carriage House and formal gardens; $335 per night.

The Deluxe Garden Room (#103): full-canopy queen feather bed; private bath; wood-burning fireplace; view of Carriage House and formal gardens; private garden entrance; $335 per night.

The Hyde Park Room (#201): full-canopy queen feather bed; private bath; wood-burning fireplace; Bay view from cushioned window couch; $395 per night.

The Padarewski Suite (#202): full-canopy queen feather bed; private bath with whirlpool tub and fireplace; wood-burning fireplace; Bay view; $675 per night.

The Green Street Room (#203): half-canopy king feather bed; private bath; $310 per night.

The Hunting Lodge Room (#301): full-canopy queen feather bed; private bath; view of Bay and Golden Gate Bridge from oversized cushion window couch; $395 per night.

The Biedermeier Suite (#302): full-canopy queen feather bed; spacious private bath with oversized Roman-style tub; Bay view; $675 per night.

The Biedermeier Room (#303): full-canopy queen feather bed; private bath; wood-burning fireplace; partial Bay view from window couch; $395 per night.
* Suite 302 and Room 303 can be combined into a two-bedroom suite.

The Sherman Suite (#401): full-canopy queen feather bed; private bath with Roman-style tub; wood-burning fireplace; private terrace with sweeping view from Golden Gate Bridge to Alcatraz Island; $700 per night.

The Pacific Heights Room (#402): half-canopy queen feather bed; private bath; wood-burning fireplace; $325 per night.

The Carriage House
The Thomas Church Garden Suite (#501): full-canopy queen feather bed; private bath; living room with free-standing fireplace; leads to garden terrace with gazebo and pond; $775 per night.

The Carriage Suite (#502): full-canopy queen feather bed; private bath; wood-burning fireplace; wet bar; refrigerator; game table; overlooks gardens; $625 per night.

The Renaissance Suite (#503): full-canopy queen feather bed; private bath; sunken living room; balcony that wraps three sides of the suite and overlooks Bay; $675 per night.

Room/suite rates: per night.	
Rooms	$310 - $395
Suites	$625 - $1,070

No pets permitted except under rare circumstances.
Smoking permitted only in formal gardens.

Member: Relais & Chateaux

Rating: Mobil Three-Star Rating (1998)

AwareNest Victorian
Bed & Breakfast

"Come to the AwareNest Victorian Bed & Breakfast, relax, and enjoy the gracious living of a bygone era."

— **Karla and Rex Hefferan, Hosts**

Guffey, named for the town 65 miles west of Colorado Springs where he was born, is the direct descendant of Smudge le Plume, who served as mayor of Guffey in the early 1990s.

Smudge was the second "bureau-cat" to be elected. Not only was Paisley the first cat elected mayor, he was the first ever mayor of Guffey. It seems that several years ago, the Park County government decided Guffey needed representation and *ordered* the town to elect a mayor. Since no one wanted the job, the cat at the general store was elected by default.

Smudge succeeded him, followed by Whiffey le Gone. The "Demo-cats" held office until unseated by "Re-pup-lican" Shanda, a Golden Retriever.

According to Karla Hefferan, Guffey's aloofness can be traced to his heritage.

"We like to tell our guests that he is aloof because he has political ties," Karla said.

Actually, Guffey, a black Persian mix, is quite friendly.

"He is often so laid back that you can hold him upside down in your arms and he will stretch way out with his head and front legs dangling," Karla said.

Having grown up on a farm, Guffey is accustomed to spending time outdoors, where he loves to roll around. After he gets covered with grass and leaves, he wants to come inside. When he does, the guestrooms are off-limits because of some guests' allergies.

Since Guffey is used to being around animals, he mingles well with Chi Wa, a Papillon, and Minnie, the Maine Coon cat, who spend much of their time in the Hefferan's residence.

Built in 1901 for a conductor with the Denver-Rio Grande Railway, this authentic Victorian home has been fully-restored with vintage stained glass windows and period antiques.

The b & b is located along the designated bike route that joins Colorado Springs to the Old Colorado City historic district. Walkers/hikers need only to step out the front door to begin their treks as well. The three-mile round trip to the majestic Garden of the Gods is well worth the effort.

The historic district is within a mile and features quaint boutiques; for the serious shopper, several malls are approximately six miles away.

Depending upon the season, tennis, golf, horseback riding, and ice skating are five miles away, cross-country skiing is 30 minutes, while downhill skiing is about a two-and-a-half hour drive.

After an hour or a day of exercising or exploring, return to the inn and relax in the outdoor hot tub. Then dine in one of the charming nearby eateries.

Guffey

AwareNest Victorian
Bed & Breakfast

1218 W. Pikes Peak Avenue
Colorado Springs, Colorado 80904
Telephone: 719-630-8241
Toll-free Reservations: 1-888-910-8241
FAX: 719-630-7467
(call phone number prior to FAXing)
E-Mail: avbb@rmi.net
Web Site: http://shell.rmi.net/~avbb
Proprietors/Hosts:
Karla and Rex Hefferan

65 miles/1 hour from Denver

Guestrooms: (1) room: private bath; telephone; television with video tape player; robes.
(1) Suite: private bath; telephone; television with video tape player; robes.

Hummingbird Room: queen bed; private bath with original clawfoot tub and hand-held shower.

Nightingale/Honeymoon Suite: queen bed; bay window; gas fireplace; private bath with marble whirlpool tub for two with separate oversized walk-in shower; decorated with turn-of-the-century photos of wedding couples.

Room/suite rates: per night; includes full breakfast featuring heart-healthy cuisine in formal dining room with wood-burning fireplace; in-suite breakfast available for extra charge; 24-hour coffee/tea service; home-baked goodies available all day; nightly turndown service.

Room and Suite	$90 - $140

Romance packages available.

No pets permitted.
Smoking permitted only on front porch.
Adult-oriented inn, but children are welcome.

Member: Bed & Breakfast Innkeepers of Colorado Association
Authentic Inns of the Pikes Peak Region
Westside Innkeepers

Holden House
1902 Bed and Breakfast Inn

"We invite you to experience 'The Romance of the Past with the Comforts of Today' in this meticulously-restored Victorian inn."

— **Sallie and Welling Clark, Hosts**

PHOTO BY SALLIE CLARK

Sallie Clark was given her first Mingtoy cat (Siamese mother and Abyssinian father) when she was a child, and these special cats have been part of her life ever since.

When the Clark's Mingtoy kitty, Sallie's fourth, disappeared in 1990, she visited the humane society daily in hopes of finding their lost pet. During one of her visits, a black/part Siamese cat was brought into the shelter along with a litter of kittens. Because she was shy, withdrawn, and older, she wasn't as likely to be adopted so Sallie thought about taking her home, but she still held out hope of finding their cat. When the Clarks did learn of their precious cat's plight, they hurried back to the shelter to adopt **Mingtoy**.

Mingtoy is kept indoors, and she is content sitting in the kitchen window watching the birds and squirrels on the backyard fence. When the Aspen Suite is unoccupied, she'll sprawl across the four-poster brass bed, peer out the window and watch the birds soar by, or lay on the carpet as the sunshine streams in.

Although Mingtoy has a playful side, she remains shy by nature and enjoys guests "on her own terms." If she's been enjoying a handmade catnip bag made especially for her by a guest from New Jersey, she'll roll all over the floor and is amenable to a tummy rub.

Mingtoy

over the warmth of the cable box on top of the television in the parlor.

"They play and chase each other," Sallie said. "It is an accepted rivalry."

Muffin, a Calico/ Siamese mix, got her name in part because she is an inn cat.

She also enjoys "walking" through the long blond hair of the b & b's assistant innkeeper, Karen Pett.

"Karen will bend over and Mingtoy will walk through her hair, back and forth, while quietly meowing," Sallie said.

Since Mingtoy had the place all to herself for two years, she was a little reticent to share it when an eight-week-old kitten was discovered abandoned in the front garden.

"Mingtoy literally pouted for six months, and for the first four months, she refused to come upstairs and even be seen with the new cat," Sallie recalled. "We were 'required' to take food down to the basement so Mingtoy would eat. But gradually, the acceptance began."

To this day, the two of them "fight for territory"

"Since she had the look of a little ragamuffin, the name 'Muffin' fit her very well," Sallie said. "Also, since we serve fresh muffins each morning here at our b & b, the name is appropriate."

Muffin loves guests, except when they try and rub her tummy. Every morning, she'll sit in the upstairs hallway and meow until at least one guest opens their door.

A Victorian Cat's Journal

Muffin

"Whichever door opens first is where she ends up," Sallie said, though like Mingtoy, she's partial to the Aspen Suite, and the following story proves it.

While guests were preparing a bubble bath, Muffin somehow got into the Aspen Suite. Before the guests had the chance to enjoy their tub for two, Muffin jumped to the side of the tub, where she proceeded to lose her balance. As she started slipping into the tub, she grabbed onto one of the plants around the edge. They both went in.

"The guests quickly came to her rescue," Sallie said. "They dried her off with a towel and placed her lovingly by the fireplace to keep warm. She was quite content with the care and attention she had received from the incident and could care less that she had 'ruined' their bubble bath, not to mention forcing them to clean the tub before they could refill it and resume their romantic evening."

When Muffin finally showed up that night, Sallie said she wondered why the cat smelled so clean and fresh.

"It remained a mystery until the story came out when our guests came down to breakfast the next morning," she said.

Since Mingtoy and Muffin are mainstays in the Main House, the Carriage House and Rose Victorian House are reserved for guests who prefer non-feline accommodations.

This Colonial Revival Victorian and Carriage House were built in 1902 by Isabel Holden, the widow of Daniel M. Holden, former rancher and prosperous Colorado Springs businessman. The Holdens held substantial mining interests in five Colorado towns and the Holden House suites reflect these town names: Aspen and Cripple Creek in the Main House; Silverton and Goldfield in the Carriage House; and Independence in the Rose Victorian House. Each suite features a bubble bath tub for two, with bubble bath among the in-suite amenities.

An eclectic collection of Victorian and traditional furnishings, along with family treasures, fills the inn. Many oriental keepsakes, which were acquired during the Clark's travels in the Navy, also are displayed.

Located in a residential neighborhood one mile west of downtown, the inn is close to all of the Pikes Peak area. A cog railroad takes visitors to the 14,110 summit. The red rocks of the

Garden of the Gods, Cheyenne Canyon Park, and Seven Falls are popular for hikes and walks; Old Colorado City and Manitou Springs invite shoppers; Royal Gorge is known for whitewater rafting; and Cripple Creek offers gambling. There's also many museums and historic sites, plus fine restaurants.

And for those who are interested in starting their own b & b inn, the Clarks offer innkeeper seminars and private consultations.

PHOTO BY JAMES VOGEL

Holden House
1902 Bed and Breakfast Inn

1102 W. Pikes Peak Avenue
Colorado Springs, Colorado 80904
Telephone: 719-471-3980
FAX: 719-471-4740
E-Mail: HoldenHouse@worldnet.att.net
Web Site: www.bbonline.com/co/holden/

Proprietors/Hosts:
Sallie and Welling Clark

60 miles/1-1/4 hours from Denver
45 miles/45 minutes from Pueblo, Colorado

Suites: (5): each with telephones; air conditioning.

Main House Suites:
Aspen Suite: four-poster, brass queen bed under open-beamed turret with hand-painted sky mural and skylight; private sitting area; see-through fireplace; private bath with oversized tub for two with separate marble shower; mountain view.

Cripple Creek Suite: white iron queen bed; private sitting room; fireplace; private bath with Roman marble tub for two and separate marble shower; mountain view.

Carriage House Suites:
Silverton Suite: four-poster, mahogany queen bed under a skylight; private sitting room; fireplace; private bath with deep marble Roman tub for two and shower combination; garden view.

Goldfield Suite: queen bed under skylight; sitting area; fireplace; private bath with deep marble Roman tub for two under skylight with hand shower; mountain view.

Adjacent Rose Victorian House:

Independence Suite: four-poster, canopy queen bed; private sitting room with bay window; fireplace; private bath with marble Roman tub for two and separate marble shower; private porch with swing; mountain view; handicapped accessible.

Suite rates: per night; based on single or double occupancy; off-season corporate rates available Sunday to Thursday for single corporate travelers only; includes full gourmet breakfast; 24-hour coffee/tea service and bottomless cookie jar.

1998: $115 - $125
1999: $120 - $135

Romance Packages available with breakfast en suite for an extra charge.

No pets permitted.
Smoking permitted only outdoors on porches.
Children not allowed.
Reservations recommended.

Member: Bed & Breakfast Innkeepers of Colorado Association
Colorado Hotel and Lodging Association
Colorado Springs Convention & Visitors Bureau
Colorado Travel & Tourism Authority
Professional Association of Innkeepers International

Rating: AAA Three Diamond Award (1998)
Mobil Three-Star Rating (1998)

The Painted Lady
Bed & Breakfast Inn

"The Painted Lady brings together a century of charm with the comforts of home."

— **Valerie and Zan Maslowski, Hosts**

Zandra had been with Valerie Maslowski for several years before Valerie became the innkeeper of The Painted Lady Bed & Breakfast Inn. Valerie said she originally planned to keep Zandra in her private residence, but that lasted only a week.

"I missed her so much that I had to include her in my innkeeping duties," Valerie said.

At night, Zandra stays in Valerie's quarters, partly to keep her out of the guestrooms in deference to guests with allergies or those who aren't cat lovers. But there's another reason why Valerie keeps Zandra with her.

"I would miss her quiet purrs in my quarters," Valerie said.

Zandra usually waits until she overhears Valerie talking to guests at check-in to make her grand entrance. At this stage in her life, this domestic short-hair with tortoiseshell coloring likes the guests to come to where she's decided to lay down, if they want to pet her.

Once an indoor/outdoor cat, Zandra now spends most of her time inside. Valerie planted a garden just outside the back door that she occasionally enjoys. But along with losing her desire to roam, she's also retired from the hunting world.

Shortly after Valerie and Zandra moved to the inn, they were sitting in the parlor when Valerie, out of the corner of her eye, thought she saw something scamper across the floor.

"I jumped up, woke my sleeping queen, explained the situation to her, and actually put her on the floor and pointed her in the right direction," Valerie recalled. "Zandra, in all her glory, stretched, yawned, and promptly jumped back on the couch to return to her nap. It was her way of telling me that her hunting days were over."

Since Valerie had to handle the situation herself, her methods proved successful and all has been right with the inn ever since.

How Zandra acquired her name is unique.

Years ago, Valerie brought two kittens from different litters into her home about a week apart. She named the male kitten, Alex, and the female became Zandra.

"I was aiming for one name for both cats," Valerie said. "In all honesty, I believe they both thought they had the same name."

Only after Alex's passing did Zandra have to learn her own name, Valerie added.

Built in 1894, this Victorian is a true painted lady on the outside. Once the family home of William Proctor, the proprietor of a local billiard hall, it also has served as a boarding house, apartments, and restaurant with upstairs gift shops. In fact, the two windows in the Suite Laura Belle that face the hallway were once the gift shop display windows.

The Painted Lady is conveniently-located between downtown Colorado Springs and the Old Colorado City historic district, making it the ideal setting for leisure or business travelers, or those who want to combine the two. Because the Painted Lady is only one block from the designated bike route, there's secure bicycle storage for those who

Zandra

PHOTO BY KAREN SCHULMAN

arrive by bike, or choose to bring theirs along.

For other sports-minded souls, there's walking/hiking in the Pikes Peak area, with the Garden of the Gods and the Cheyenne Canyon Park popular destinations; tennis; golf; horseback riding at the Garden of the Gods, the Broadmoor, and for those who want a mountain setting, Ute Pass; fly and lake fishing (about 30 minutes away); ice skating at the World Arena; and skiing (cross-country about 30 to 45 minutes away and downhill about a two-hour drive).

One of the newest features of the b & b is the outdoor hot tub and deck, a wonderful place to watch the sunset reflected in the clouds of Pikes Peak. Guests can pre-reserve the hot tub for 45 minutes of private use.

Many restaurants are nearby, and if you decide to make an evening of dinner and dancing, Valerie may even help you with your two-step. Don't forget to pack your cowboy boots or get a pair while you're here. The Old Colorado City historic district is known for its boutiques, as well as its antique shops and galleries.

The Painted Lady Bed & Breakfast Inn

1318 West Colorado Avenue
Colorado Springs, Colorado 80904
Telephone: 719-473-3165
Toll-free Reservations: 1-800-370-3165
FAX: 719-635-1396
E-Mail: paintedladyinn@worldnet.att.net
Web Site:
www.bbonline.com/co/paintedlady/

Proprietors/Hosts:
Valerie and Zan Maslowski

60 miles/1 hour from Denver
75 miles/1-1/2 hours from Denver International Airport
15 miles/25 minutes from Colorado Springs Muni Airport

Guestrooms: (2): each with private bath; in-room telephone.
(2) Suites: each with private bath; in-room telephone.

Lily's Lookout: queen bed; private bath with shower; accommodates two people.

Violet's Garden: queen bed; private bath with two-person soaking tub and shower; accommodates two people.

Suite Laura Belle: two-room suite with queen bed; private bath with oversized clawfoot tub and hand-held shower; remote-controlled gas fireplace; can accommodate up to four people.

A Suite Retreat: three-room suite; two bedrooms, each with queen bed; sitting area with twin bed, television and video cassette recorder; private bath with tub and shower; small kitchen; can accommodate up to five people; also available for weekly rentals.

Room/suite rates: per night; based on double occupancy; add $15 for each additional person in suite; reduced winter rates may be available, depending on length of stay or special promotion; includes full breakfast served in the dining room; for those with early departures, "to go" breakfast is available; 24-hour coffee/tea service; never-ending supply of cookies.

Lily's Lookout	$85 - $110
Violet's Garden	$95 - $115
Suite Laura Belle	$110 - $130
A Suite Retreat	$110 - $135

No pets permitted.
Smoking permitted only outside.
Children over age 4 can be accommodated only in the suites.
Advance reservations recommended.

Member: Authentic Inns of the Pikes Peak Region
Bed & Breakfast Innkeepers of Colorado
Association
Colorado Springs Convention & Visitors Bureau
Colorado Travel and Tourism Authority
Old Colorado City Historical Society
Westside Innkeepers Association

Wild Lane
Bed & Breakfast Inn

"Whether you're wandering through the gardens or indulging in the ambiance of my grandfather's home, you're sure to enjoy your stay with us."

— **Lanette and Steven Wild, Hosts**

When Steven Wild moved back to the home his grandfather built in 1905, naturally his cat **Ollie** came with him. Steven selected Ollie's name simply because he liked it. This half Burmese-half Tabby is guest-friendly and likes to "talk" to guests, if only to tell them where his food is kept. His passion for eating is evident, especially if he happens to fall asleep on your chest.

"Try and continue to breathe. He weighs 17 pounds!" said Lanette Wild.

Ollie also has a unique morning wake-up call.

"Ollie has been known to go to guests' closed doors in the morning and 'head-butt' the door, which sounds amazingly like someone is knocking. Guests think it is and answer 'Yes?'" Lanette said.

She said Ollie's mission is to be petted. Or maybe it's to tell those guests he might have missed where to find his food...

Bubba, the kitten of an adopted stray, joined the Wild Lane Bed & Breakfast family in 1997. Once again, Steven named him because he liked the name.

Bubba's mother now lives with a family in Ft. Collins, Colorado. So far, thankfully, Bubba hasn't inherited his mother's "taste" for wedding cake and weddings.

"Bubba's mother, Annie, particularly enjoyed weddings — 'entertaining' guests by helping herself to wedding cake before anyone else, and certainly without being asked, not to mention waltzing the length of a lovely white linen banquet table with muddy paws," Lanette said. "So far, Bubba seems better behaved!"

Ollie

"It's the guests who bring them to their rooms," Lanette added.

Nestled in the foothills of the Rocky Mountains, the Wild Lane Bed & Breakfast Inn is an elegant country mansion and the former home of Steven Wild's grandfather. In addition to the five bedrooms, furnished with turn-of-the-century antiques, the landmark house features three fireplaces, living and dining room, parlor, library, and enclosed sunporch, from which guests might glimpse the inn's "resident" wildlife — squirrels, rabbits, raccoons, and deer.

Bubba, which Lanette describes as a "white Heinz 57," shares Steven's interest in herbs. He likes to follow guests to the greenhouse and extensive herb farm that Steven has planted, which are used for both culinary and crafting purposes.

Bubba also likes to hunt and climb trees, and when it comes to being outdoors, Lanette describes both cats as "opportunists."

"When the door is open, they come and go as they like," Lanette said.

"Officially," however, they are not supposed to come and go into the guestrooms, but some of the blame rests on guests' shoulders.

Steven's pride-and-joy is his herb farm, and many of the gourmet breakfast creations have a distinctly herbal flair.

The town of Loveland is known for its antique shops and bronze sculpture studios. Guests are

Bubba

encouraged to borrow a bike from the b & b or set out on foot to go shopping or exploring the extensive trail system.

Trout fishing is nearby in the Big Thompson River; also nearby are tennis, golf, horseback riding, ice skating, and cross-country skiing, depending on the season. For those in the mood for a drive, Rocky Mountain National Park is just 45 minutes away while downhill skiing is a two-hour ride.

Wild Lane
Bed & Breakfast Inn

5445 Wild Lane
Loveland, Colorado 80538
Telephone: 970-669-0303
Toll-free Reservations: 1-800-204-3320
FAX: --
E-Mail: wildlane@info2000.net
Web Site:
www.bbonline.com/co/wildlane
Proprietors/Hosts:
Lanette and Steven Wild

50 miles/1 hour from Denver
5 miles/10 minutes from Loveland, Colorado

Guestrooms: (4) rooms: each with private bath; air-conditioning.
(1) Suite: private bath; air-conditioning.

Pink Rose Room: queen bed; private bath with tub and shower; sitting area and writing desk; view of Rocky Mountains; $89 per night.

Red Rose Room: queen bed; private bath; writing desk; south view; $89 per night.

Yellow Rose Room: king sleigh bed; private bath with tub and shower; sitting area and writing desk; west view of Rocky Mountains; $89 per night.

Wild Rose Room: full bed; private bath; writing desk; $89 per night.

Blue Rose Suite: mahogany queen clawfoot bed; private bath with shower and separate whirlpool tub; sitting area and writing desk; view of Devils Backbone rock formation; $109 per night.

Room/suite rates: per night; single or double occupancy; $15 extra per additional guest; includes full gourmet breakfast, which can be delivered to guestroom upon request.

Rooms	$89
Suite	$109

No pets permitted.
Smoking permitted only outside.
Children age 15 and older are welcome.

Member: Professional Association of Innkeepers International
Bed & Breakfast Innkeepers of Colorado Association

Crystal Dreams
Bed & Breakfast

"This is our dream come true and we wish to share this experience with you."

— **Lisa and Stephen Wagner, Hosts**

 **Akala Ihu** and **Ele Ihu** were adopted by Lisa and Steve Wagner at an animal rights movement at the University of Hawaii when they were students in 1990. Given the cats' birthplace, it was only fitting that these twin brothers take Hawaiian names. Born on Oahu, Hawaii, Akala Ihu means *pink nose,* while the literal translation for Ele Ihu is *black nose.* And if it weren't for their different colored noses, even the Wagners would have a difficult time telling them apart!

These tuxedo kitties traveled with Lisa and Steve to Colorado and are now the resident cats at the Crystal Dreams Bed & Breakfast. The cats enjoy indoor/outdoor privileges, but are not allowed in the guest-rooms.

Upon check-in, guests are likely to be greeted by Ele, the more social of the b & b's social directors.

"Ele loves our guests and shows them much affection and entertainment," Lisa said. "Akala is a bit more shy, but will visit with guests outside the b & b."

Both cats are quite enamored with water. Maybe it has something to do with being born on a tropical island! Ele loves to drink it, be sprayed with the hose, or lounge in the Wagner's clawfoot tub.

Akala also likes the bathroom. Approximately seven years ago, Lisa was reading and her husband, Steve, was away, when she heard "someone" using the commode. Imagine her surprise — and relief — when she discovered it was Akala.

"He loves to use the toilet," Lisa said. "I *never* encouraged this behavior."

Crystal Dreams Bed & Breakfast, a romantic country Victorian, is nestled between majestic red cliffs and the Crystal River in Redstone, Colorado, a historical community and mining town known as the "Ruby of the Rockies." Built specifically as a bed & breakfast by Steve, its riverfront setting and the living room fireplace add to its romantic ambiance. While enjoying home-baked goodies, guests might glimpse Bighorn sheep, deer, or Canadian geese.

Fly fishing is just outside the back door. The area also affords sports enthusiasts bicycling, tennis, golf, horseback riding, downhill and cross-country skiing, as well as walking/hiking options.

Shops and galleries abound in town, filled with treasures by Colorado artists.

Ele Ihu and Akala Ihu

Crystal Dreams Bed & Breakfast

0475 Redstone Boulevard
Redstone, Colorado 81623
Telephone: 970-963-8240
FAX: 970-963-8882
E-Mail: redstone@rof.net
Web Site:
www.net-unlimited.com/crystaldreams

Proprietors/Hosts:
Lisa and Stephen Wagner

180 miles/3-1/2 hours from Denver
50 miles/45 minutes from Aspen, Colorado

Guestrooms: (3)

Moon River Room: king bed; private bath with two-person claw-foot tub; view of Crystal River.

Bighorn Room: queen bed; private bath with two-person claw-foot tub; view of majestic mountains.

Mt. Casa Room: queen and twin bed; private bath with shower.

Room rates: per night; based on double occupancy; $10 per night discount for single occupancy; 10% discount for 5 days or more; includes full gourmet breakfast served by candlelight. Breakfast in bed is served upon request.

Monday - Thursday	$90
Friday - Sunday & Holidays	$100

No pets permitted.
Non-smoking property.
Children over age 12 are welcome; not suitable for
small children.
Reservations encouraged.
Open year-round; Redstone truly is a village for all seasons.

Member: Bed & Breakfast Association of Colorado

The Grandison at Maney Park

 One day in August 1989, The Grandison was hosting a "white elephant" auction when a stray cat appeared for the first time. With all the bidding and offering going on, surely someone would offer to take this precious possession home. But as friendly as she was, at the end of the day she remained. So Claudia Wright took her in, making sure she didn't starve for affection or nourishment. She stayed around for a few weeks, then disappeared.

Three months later, she was back. Claudia thought the onset of cold weather might have prompted her return. However, she learned the real reason in February when the stray gave birth to four kittens — three males and a female.

Interestingly, the day before the kittens came into this world, a young woman from Norway who was staying at The Grandison was fascinated by the "kittens in the cat's tummy."

"Mocci was the name of the young lady," Claudia said. "The day after she checked out, the cat had her kittens. We named the one female kitten, Mocci, after her."

This mixed breed with tortoise-shell markings and six toes is quite vocal and uses her voice to get attention, as an unrequested wake-up call, and even to steal center stage from a bride-to-be.

"We were having a wedding and when the soloist began singing, Mocci walked right in the middle of all the guests, stood in front of the soloist, and vocalized along with the singer," Claudia recalled.

Mocci spends about half of her time out-of-doors. If invited, she will gladly take a guest up on their offer to join them in their guestroom.

"She loves to snoop in guests' luggage," Claudia said.

When it's time for guests to check-out, if they can't bear to say good-bye to Mocci, there's no need to despair. One of The Grandison's other guests felt the same way and created "Snuggle Stones" — a stone painted with Mocci's picture that bears a remarkable resemblance to the resident cat. They are available in the b & b's gift shop.

"It looks like a miniature Mocci you can hold in your hand," said Claudia.

That, along with the memories one holds in their heart, just might tide them over until their next stay at The Grandison at Maney Park.

 Built in 1904, this historic home was moved one mile to its present location five years later, never disturbing the original Philippine mahogany woodwork, stained and leaded glass, curved staircase, carved banister and cozy alcoves. Renovation of this three-story, nine-room inn restored its elegant Victorian features while adding luxurious amenities to the guestrooms that include private baths, whirlpool tubs, and fireplaces.

The Grandison at Maney Park is conveniently-located near downtown Oklahoma City, which makes it a popular honeymoon spot, gathering place for family and friends, as well as locale for business meetings and retreats, group functions and receptions.

Among the popular nearby destinations are the Cowboy Hall of Fame; Frontier City, an Old West amusement park; and the Old Bricktown/Warehouse District. Within walking distance are two museums, once the private residences

Mocci

of local oil barons. The athletically-inclined can avail themselves of nearby golf and tennis, as well as the inn's on-site exercise equipment.

The bed & breakfast also features a gift shop complete with antiques, collectibles, handcrafted items and a large selection of made-in-Oklahoma products.

The Grandison at Maney Park

1200 N. Shartel
Oklahoma City, Oklahoma 73103
Telephone: 405-232-8778
Toll-free Reservations: 1-800-240-4667
FAX: 405-232-5039
E-Mail: Grandison@Juno.com
Web Site:
www.bbonline.com/ok/grandison/index.html

Proprietor/Host:
Claudia Wright

7 miles/12 minutes from Oklahoma City Will Rogers World Airport

Guestrooms: (7) rooms: each with telephones and computer lines.
(2) suites: each with telephones and computer lines.

Hunter and Hound: black wrought-iron queen bed; private bath; $105 weekdays; $125 weekends.

Florence's Room: late 1800s high-back Victorian bed with tapestry canopy; palatial corner whirlpool tub; private bath with shower; $105 weekdays; $125 weekends.

Divine Providence: king bed with feather mattress; whirlpool tub for two; private bath; $115 weekdays; $135 weekends.

Royal Retreat: double bed surrounded by bay windows; private bath; $75 weekdays and weekends.

Memory Cove: one-of-a-kind, mahogany canopy queen bed; whirlpool tub for two; private bath with shower; $110 weekdays; $130 weekends.

Anna Augusta: dark oak queen bed; triangular-shaped whirlpool tub; private bath with pedestal sink and shower; $110 weekdays; $130 weekends.

Safari: wrought-iron and wicker queen bed; decorated loft area; large private bath with shower; first-floor private entrance; handicapped accessible; $85 weekdays and weekends.

Jim Bob: Western/railroad theme and rustic feel; whirlpool tub; private bath; $90 weekdays; $110 weekends. For an additional $15, guests can use a wicker sitting area.

Treehouse Hideaway: queen bed resembles a hammock; elevated whirlpool tub positioned under an original skylight; private bath; room painted by a local artist with a white-washed fence, blue sky with clouds, and stars that glow in the dark; $90 weekdays; $110 weekends. For an additional $15, guests can use a wicker sitting area.

Room/suite rates: per night; corporate rates and extended stay discounts available; includes expanded continental breakfast served in upstairs guest refreshment area; on weekends, full breakfast served in downstairs dining room; breakfast delivered to guestrooms upon request.

	Weekdays	Weekends
Rooms	$75 - $115	$75 - $135
Suites	$105	$125

Pet-friendly.
Non-smoking property.
Reservations recommended.

Member: Professional Association of Innkeepers International
         Oklahoma Bed and Breakfast Association
         American Historic Inns

CANADA

Beacon Bed and Breakfast

"The Beacon Bed and Breakfast offers amenities conducive to relaxation and well-being. We offer a library of self-help books as well as the opportunity to experience massage sessions guaranteed to leave you relaxed."

— Shirley and Roger Randall, Hosts

Nothing could possibly rival a person's passion for their pet. But if anything could come close, it might be their love affair with their automobile. So it's no wonder that the Randalls combined the two.

"**Jetty** is our cat's name," explained Shirley. "We owned a Volkswagon Jetta diesel at the time of her arrival. Her purr reminded us of our car motor."

In fact, it was a car that brought Jetty and the Randalls together in the first place. One day when Shirley drove her daughter to work at the Wildlife Santuary, a two-month-old kitty greeted them upon arrival. Someone had left her there, and her lovely purr convinced the caretaker to keep her until he could find a caring home. Shirley told them to keep looking. Somehow, the kitten with the unique tortoise-shell coloring got into the car. And the rest, as they say, is history.

"She is now our most spoiled possession," Shirley said.

Jetty's fascination with cars didn't end with Shirley's, however.

"One of our guests arrived home after a canoe trip. Jetty had apparently jumped into the back of the truck and hid under the canoe. Luckily, the gentleman at the canoe rental place took the canoe out of his truck when he got to his place of business, only to find a very scared pussy cat cuddled in the corner of the truck," Shirley said. "We were so glad that she hadn't jumped out somewhere en route."

If guests happen to leave their car doors open, Jetty will jump inside to inspect. While she may not always like what she finds, Jetty likes most guests, except for children who terrify her. If she finds an empty adult lap, she'll take a chance that they're a cat lover. She also likes to lay in the high-traffic area, hoping someone will stop, bend down, and pet her.

While Jetty is not the only reason that guests enjoy the Beacon Bed and Breakfast, they certainly look for her immediately upon arrival.

"Our previous brochure stated 'friendly cat to greet you,'" Shirley said. "So when we opened our door, guests would say 'oh, there's the friendly cat who greets you.'"

Jetty

She has indoor/outdoor privileges. But even with her beautiful, thick coat, she prefers to stay inside during the cooler months.

"Most people aren't affected by her presence, even if they have allergies to cats," Shirley remarked. "But just to be on the safe side, Jetty is not allowed in the guestrooms."

"They could care less about who we are!" Shirley said jokingly. "It's enough to give the average host and hostess a complex!"

 If total relaxation and rejuvenation is what you are looking for, look no further than the Beacon Bed and Breakfast. With its incredible, unrestricted, panoramic view of the Malaspina Strait facing Vancouver Island and its calming, waterfront location, this home-away-from-home is the purr-fect place to unwind and find peace and serenity.

Two of the more popular guest amenities include the soothing hot tub that overlooks the Strait of Georgia. It's also the best place to catch the sunset in the fall or summer months. Another is the relaxing Massage and Healing Touch sessions available from Shirley, a Massage Technician and Healing Touch Practitioner.

"This is guaranteed to provide the rest you deserve," Shirley said.

The b & b's "resident eagles," so named because they entertain the guests approximately 10 months out of the year, usually can be enjoyed from the dining room.

For those looking to explore the area, days can be filled with walking/hiking, fishing, kayaking, canoeing, water skiing, diving, bicycling, tennis, golf, horseback riding, birdwatching, beachcombing, and sightseeing — just to name a few of the available activities. For those who want to explore the "old town" of Powell River, British Columbia, there's a self-guided Heritage Walk that takes approximately one hour.

Restaurants are close by, but for guests who prefer to eat in, the b & b's kitchen is available to prepare a quiet dinner. All the owners ask is that you be sure to leave the facilities as immaculate as you found them.

Beacon Bed and Breakfast

3750 Marine Avenue
Powell River, British Columbia,
Canada V8A 2H8
Telephone: 604-485-5563
FAX: 604-485-9450
E-Mail: --
Web Site: www.vancouver-bc.com/beaconbb/

Proprietors/Hosts:
Shirley and Roger Randall

2 ferry rides/cruises and 1-1/2 hour easy drive/5-1/2 hours from Vancouver, British Columbia

Guestrooms: (3)

Sunrise Room: queen bed; adjacent bath; telephone; shares living room with view of water and snowcapped mountains of Vancouver Island.

Serenity Ensuite: queen and twin bed; private bath; telephone; shares living room with view of water and snowcapped mountains of Vancouver Island.

Sunset Suite: queen and twin bed; private bath with shower; telephone; television; adjoining sitting area that can double as a bedroom; gas fireplace; can accommodate up to six guests; wheelchair accessible.

Room/suites rates: per night; includes full breakfast. Guests' particular dietary needs accommodated whenever possible.

	May 1 - September 30	October 1 - April 30
Sunrise Room	Single: $75 Double: $85	Single: $60 Double: $65
Serenity Ensuite	Single: $85 Double: $95 Extra Person: $20	Single: $65 Double: $75 Extra Person: $20
Sunset Suite	Single: $125 Double: $125 Each extra person: $20	Single: $95 Double: $95 Each extra person: $20

Small pets permitted only in Sunset Suite.
Smoking permitted only on outside porches.
Adult-oriented; children over age 12 are welcome.
Reservations encouraged.

Member: British Columbia Government Accommodation
Guide
Western Canadian Bed & Breakfast and
Innkeepers Association

Penny Farthing Inn

Friskie was such a whirlwind as a kitten that the name Friskie fit purrfectly. He's slowed down somewhat, especially of late because Fluffy, the granddam inn cat, was tragically taken from their lives in July 1998. Friskie is a lap cat, a trait he inherited from Fluffy, but he selects the lucky lap. When not lap-sitting, he's sitting on the piano bench playing the piano or curled up in the pot by the front steps.

"Friskie may play the piano for guests as he has on TV," said Lyn Hainstock.

Friskie's musical talents aside, guests will quickly discover that music is an integral part of the Penny Farthing stay, with the parlor piano encouraging personal expression. The entertainment center with its CDs and tapes also helps guests to relive past moments and make new memories.

When one of Lyn's daughters gave her sister a cat as a gift, the name Harmony struck a cord with everyone. When Harmony gave birth in 1993, **Melody** became the newest resident cat. She makes her own kind of music "talking" a mile a minute.

Friskie

Hendrix, who also arrived in 1993, was named for Jimi Hendrix, the musician. He is more comfortable around the guests than he is with his feline family since they haven't made him feel particularly welcome.

Melody

All three cats can frequently be found on the inn's delightful front porch as well as in their favorite places in the common areas of the house. However, guestrooms are strictly off-limits, and those guests in Lucinda's Room should heed the sign to keep the adjacent bathroom door closed at all times or else they may find they're not alone with their thoughts when nature calls.

Hendrix

Penny Farthing Inn, a 1912 heritage house with original stained glass windows, is located just five minutes from downtown Vancouver in the vibrant Kitsilano district. Guests can bike, walk, hike, or hop a bus to the beach and parks (some with tennis courts), as well as shops, restaurants, and the University of British Columbia.

Depending on the season, guests will find golf, horseback riding, and ice skating a 10- to 15-minute drive. For downhill skiing, plan on 25 minutes to reach the local slopes while Whistler is about two hours away, with great skiing and some spectacular cross-country ski trails.

The guest lounge with its gas fireplace offers a large selection of CDs and tapes. The lounge also features a piano for those who prefer to make their own music or entertain others, plus a games table complete with cards, puzzles, and games.

For the literary-minded, books abound around the inn. Titles range from best-selling novels to picturesque coffee-table books.

The inn also features a business center equipped with a computer, e-mail connection, printer, photocopier, and FAX machine.

Penny Farthing Inn

2855 West 6th Avenue
Vancouver, British Columbia, Canada
V6K 1X2
Telephone: 604-739-9002
FAX: 604-739-9004
E-Mail: farthing@uniserve.com
Web Site: www.pennyfarthinginn.com
Proprietor/Host:
Lyn Hainstock

175 - 200 miles/3 hours from Seattle, Washington
20 - 25 minutes from B.C. Capital Airport
30 miles/2-1/2 hours by ferry from Victoria, British Columbia

Guestrooms: (2): (1) with private bath in room; (1) with private bath adjacent to room.
(2) Suites: each with private bath en suite.

Abigail's Suite: queen brass bed; private bath with bath, shower and skylights; sitting room with sofa bed; television; video cassette recorder, stereo, and CD player; telephone; refrigerator; tea/coffeemaker; views of mountains, city, and water; suite occupies entire top floor; $100 USD, single; $122 USD, double; $135 CAD, single; $165 CAD, double.

Bettina's Suite: four-poster pine bed; private bath with shower; sitting room with gas fireplace, television, video cassette recorder, stereo, and CD player; telephone; refrigerator; tea/coffeemaker; veranda with partial mountain views overlooking garden; $100 USA, single; $111 USA, double; $135 CAD, single; $150 CAD, double.

Lucinda's Room: king or twin brass bed; private bath with shower adjacent to room; telephone; overlooks front garden; $70 USD, single; $81 USD, double; $95 CAD, single; $110 CAD, double.

Sophie's Room: four-poster pine bed; private bath with shower; telephone; porch overlooking front garden; $70 USD, single; $81 USD, double; $95 CAD, single; $110 CAD, double.

Room/suite rates: per night; includes full breakfast served in dining room overlooking English country garden; weather-permitting, breakfast also served in the garden; also can be served in Abigail's Suite or Bettina's Suite; continental breakfast available for early risers. Coffee/tea/cookies available day-long in the self-serve Butler's Pantry.

	US Dollars		Canadian Dollars	
	Single	Double	Single	Double
Rooms	$70	$81	$95	$110
Suites	$100	$111 & $122	$135	$150 & $165

No pets permitted.
Smoking permitted only outside.

Member: Tourism Vancouver/Tourism Vancouver Coast & Mountain
Western Canada Bed & Breakfast Innkeepers Association

UNITED KINGDOM

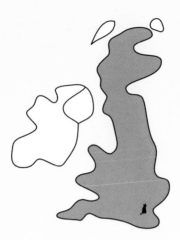

England
London
 — The Pembridge Court Hotel, 158-161

The Pembridge Court Hotel

"The Pembridge Court Hotel is renowned for its warm, personal service. We really do enjoy looking after our guests."

— **Valerie Gilliat, General Manager**

PEMBRIDGE
COURT HOTEL

While guests are likely to spot media personalities and famous musicians, who are among The Pembridge Court Hotel's loyal clientele, the real stars are **Spencer** and **Churchill**. These two orange tabbies or Marmalade cats (called Ginger Moggie in the U.K.) have appeared in print as well as on the tele. Spencer even has a recurring role in the new series "Madsen" with Ian McShane on the BBCI. Churchill has been photographed with a number of well-known people, since he regards the sitting room as his own and it frequently is used as a backdrop for photo shoots and interviews.

While every cat is a star in his or her own right, maybe these two will share their secret of success in exchange for a tummy rub...or two.

Spencer arrived at the hotel in 1988 as a companion for Pembridge, the property's first resident cat. When Pemmy died in 1990, Churchill carried on the tradition of having two ginger cats.

Spencer was so named because of an award given to the hotel the previous year by Countess Spencer, Princess Diana's stepmother. And since the Spencer-Churchills are among the most famous of British families, it was only fitting that the newest addi-

Spencer and Churchill

tion to the Pembridge family take the name of Churchill.

Spencer is the chief "meeter and greeter," spending a lot of time on the front reception desk. Churchill is the "bellboy" since he adores riding in the lift (elevator). Both cats go outdoors whenever they wish, and given any encourage-ment, spend time in the guestrooms.

"They are both immensely popular with our guests and have admirers all over the world," said Valerie Gilliat. "Spencer and Churchill are such an important part of the hotel it simply would not be the same place without them."

"We are absolutely cat mad here and so are most of our guests!" she added.

Spencer and Churchill also raise funds for charity through their own lapel pins. According to Valerie, 50 pence of each one sold benefits either the Royal Society for the Preven-tion of Cruelty to Animals or the Great Ormond Street Children's Hospital.

"They have already collected quite a lot of money," Valerie said.

The Pembridge Court Hotel is situated in Notting Hill Gate, with its "one-off" or unusual shops, great pubs and restaurants, garden square, and the largest antique market in the world on nearby Portobello Road. This Victorian town house also is close to Hyper Hyper Arcade, where up-and-coming designers showcase and sell their latest creations. It's also a short taxi ride to Harrods!

A short walk or run will bring you to Hyde Park with its Serpentine Lake for swimming or boating; Rotten Row for horseback rides and walks; Kensington Gardens; and the Wildlife Gardens of Holland Park.

If you still have any energy left, the hotel offers a specially-priced day membership at the exclusive Lambton Place Health Club. Spa treatments and salon services also are available at preferred prices.

Another of the hotel's drawing cards is the cozy and informal Caps Restaurant and Cellar Bar. The hotel also offers 24-hour roomservice.

Guests who enjoy Victoriana will appreciate the collection of fans, purses, dresses, and gloves which add to the hotel's residential feel.

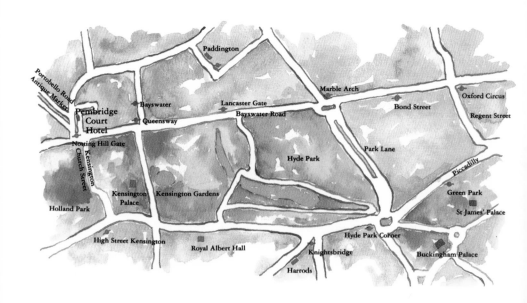

The Pembridge Court Hotel

34 Pembridge Gardens
London, UK W2 4DX
Telephone Outside U.K.: 011 44 171 229 9977
Telephone Inside U.K.: 0171 229 9977
FAX Outside U.K.: 011 44 171 727 4982
FAX Toll-free in U.S.: 1-800-709-9882
FAX Inside U.K.: 0171 727 4982
E-Mail: --
Web Site: --

Owner:
Richard Lim
General Manager (on site):
Valerie Gilliat

14 miles/45 minutes by taxi from London Heathrow Airport

Guestrooms: (6) standard: each with direct-dial telephones; satellite television; private bath with Molton Brown toiletries; hair dryer and trouser press.

(14) deluxe: each with direct-dial telephones; satellite television and video facilities; sofa/seating area; private bath with Molton Brown toiletries; hair dryer and trouser press.

Room rates: per night; based on double occupancy; includes full English breakfast, which can be delivered to the guestroom upon request; also includes Value Added Tax (VAT).

Standard, Single Room	110 British Pounds
Deluxe, Single Room	135 - 145 British Pounds
Standard, Twin Rooms	135 British Pounds
Deluxe Twin, Double Room	165 - 175 British Pounds

Pet-friendly.
Smoking permitted only in designated guestrooms and in public areas.

Member: British Hospitality Association

REMEMBRANCE

We lovingly remember those faithful resident cats who are no longer here to greet guests and stand by their innkeeper's side. And never far from our thoughts are every cat who, no matter how briefly, touched our lives and changed us forever.

ABOUT THE AUTHOR

Susan Bard Hall is a free-lance writer who has written hundreds of articles about hotels, travel destinations, and cats.

Her byline has appeared in over 25 consumer and trade publications, including *Cat Fancy, CATsumer Report, Historic Traveler, Hotel & Motel Management Magazine,* and the *Chicago Tribune.*

Ms. Hall is a member of the Cat Writers' Association and the National Writers Association.

She and her husband, Norman, and step-cat, Taj, reside in the Chicago-area.

INDEX

INDEX

Georgia
Jekyll Island
— *The Jekyll Island Club Hotel:*
Jekyll, born April 1997; 50-53

Idaho
Sandpoint
— *The Coit House Bed & Breakfast:*
Dollar, born 1995; Jerry, born 1995;
and Tommy, born 1995; 92-94

Massachusetts
West Yarmouth, Cape Cod
— *The Manor House Bed & Breakfast:*
Whitesocks, born March 1991; and
Hairball, born March 1992; 4-7

Michigan
Big Bay
— *Big Bay Point Lighthouse Bed & Breakfast:*
Max, born May or June 1990; and
Sidney, born April 1996; 70-73
South Haven
— *A Country Place Bed and Breakfast and Cottages:*
Munchkin, born 1989; and
Miss Patience, born Spring 1994; 74-78
Vassar
— *The North House:*
Harley Davidson, born 1992; and
Black Beauty, born 1998; 80-83

Minnesota
Wabasha
— *The Anderson House:*
R.B., a.k.a. Arby, born 1987; Buttons, born 1988;
Arnold, born 1989; Mickey, born 1991;
Fred, born 1992; Goblin, born 1992;
Tiger, born 1992; Ginger, born 1994;
Max, born 1995; Midnight, born 1995; and
Bambie, born 1997; 84-89

New Jersey
Belmar
— *The Seaflower — A Bed and Breakfast Inn:*
Mr. Muggs, born 1994; and
Señor Pesto, born 1995; 8-10
Cape May
— *The Albert Stevens Inn & Cat's Garden:*
42 cats including Billy, born July 1984;
Luke, born July 1991; Martha, born August 1997;
Mickey, born August 1997; and
Derek, born June 1998; 12-17

North Carolina
Marshall
— *Marshall House Bed & Breakfast Inn:*
Lady, born 1981; Bashful, born April 1992;
Dusty, born April 1992; Blizzard, born 1993 (?);
JoJo, born 1994; Daniella, born 1995;
Sherlock, born 1995; Watson, born 1995;
Bobo Rockefeller, born 1996; Casper, born 1996 (?);
Jasmine, born 1996 (?); Tigger, born 1996;
Angel, born 1997; DoDo, born 1997;
Gracie, born 1997; and Tip, born 1997; 54-62

Oklahoma
Oklahoma City
— *The Grandison at Maney Park:*
Mocci, born 1990; 142-145

Oregon
Newport
— *The Sylvia Beach Hotel:*
Stella New Jersey, born 1998; 96-99

Pennsylvania
Bradford
— *Glendorn, A Lodge in the Country:*
Reggie, born 1992; 18-21
Jacobus (York)
— *Past Purr-fect Bed and Breakfast:*
Simba, the Lion King, born July 1996; 22-23
Newtown
— *Hollileif Bed & Breakfast:*
Furguson, born December 1988; and
Jenny, born December 1996; 24-27

South Carolina

Union

— *The Inn at Merridun:*
J.D. (Jefferson Davis, a.k.a. Just A Darn Cat),
born September 1991; 64-67

Vermont

Brandon

— *The Churchill House Inn:*
Audrey, born July 1986; 28-29
— *The Lilac Inn:*
Sebastian, born 1990; and
White Darling, born 1990; 30-32

Manchester Center

— *Manchester Highlands Inn:*
Humphrey, born 1987; 34-36

Canada — British Columbia

Powell River

— *Beacon Bed and Breakfast:*
Jetty, born 1988; 148-151

Vancouver

— *Penny Farthing Inn:*
Friskie, born 1985; Hendrix, born 1993;
and Melody, born 1993; 152-155

United Kingdom — England

London

— *The Pembridge Court Hotel:*
Spencer, born June 1988; and
Churchill, born June 1990; 158-161

LISTING FORM

If you've stayed at a purr-fect place not included in this book or know of one and feel it should be included in the next edition of *PURR-FECT PLACES TO STAY:* Bed & Breakfasts, Country Inns, and Hotels with Resident Cats by Susan Bard Hall, please complete this listing form and mail to:

Letters Etcetera
P.O. Box 811280
Chicago, IL 60681-1280

Thank you in advance for your interest in *PURR-FECT PLACES TO STAY.*

Name of Bed & Breakfast, Country Inn, or Hotel with Resident Cat(s):

_____

Address: _____

City: _____

State: _____ Zip Code: _____

Telephone Number: (_____) _____

E-Mail Address: _____

Providing your name and address is optional. But if you provide your name and this listing is included in the next edition, as a way of saying thanks, I'll send along a complimentary copy of the new edition when it's published.

Name: _____

Company Name (if applicable): _____

Address: _____

City: _____

State: _____ Zip Code: _____

Telephone Number: (_____) _____

E-Mail Address: _____

ORDER FORM

I would like to order *PURR-FECT PLACES TO STAY:* **Bed & Breakfasts, Country Inns, and Hotels with Resident Cats.**

Telephone Orders: Use Visa or MasterCard and call 312-938-1137. (8 a.m. – 7 p.m. Central Time.)

FAX Orders: Use Visa or MasterCard and FAX order form to 312-938-1913.

Postal Orders: Enclose check or money order made payable to **Letters Etcetera**. Or use Visa or MasterCard. Mail order form to: Letters Etcetera, P.O. Box 811280, Chicago, IL 60681-1280.

Questions? Call 312-938-1137 or e-mail to bkdu67a@prodigy.com.

PURR-FECT PLACES TO STAY (U.S. Only)	**$19.95**
Postage and Handling (U.S. Only)	**$ 4.25**
Sales Tax (Illinois Residents Only)	**$ 1.75**
SUB-TOTAL	$____.____

_____**books ordered @ $____.____ each = $_____._____**

TOTAL ENCLOSED

❏ **Check**   ❏ **Money Order**   ❏ [VISA]   ❏ [MasterCard]

Card #:_____**Exp. Date:**_____

Name on card:_____

Signature:_____

Please send the book(s) to:

Name: _____

Company Name (if applicable): _____

Address: _____

City: _____

State: _____ **Zip Code:** _____

Daytime Telephone: _____

Autographed copy to: _____

Autographed copy to: _____

ORDER FORM

I would like to order *PURR-FECT PLACES TO STAY:* **Bed & Breakfasts, Country Inns, and Hotels with Resident Cats.**

Telephone Orders: Use Visa or MasterCard and call 312-938-1137. (8 a.m. – 7 p.m. Central Time.)

FAX Orders: Use Visa or MasterCard and FAX order form to 312-938-1913.

Postal Orders: Enclose check or money order made payable to **Letters Etcetera**. Or use Visa or MasterCard. Mail order form to: Letters Etcetera, P.O. Box 811280, Chicago, IL 60681-1280.

Questions? Call 312-938-1137 or e-mail to bkdu67a@prodigy.com.

PURR-FECT PLACES TO STAY (U.S. Only)	**$19.95**
Postage and Handling (U.S. Only)	**$ 4.25**
Sales Tax (Illinois Residents Only)	**$ 1.75**
SUB-TOTAL	$.

_____**books ordered @ $**____.____ **each = $**_____._____

TOTAL ENCLOSED

❏ **Check**   ❏ **Money Order**   ❏ *VISA*   ❏ *MasterCard*

Card #:_____ **Exp. Date:**_____

Name on card:_____

Signature:_____

Please send the book(s) to:

Name: _____

Company Name (if applicable): _____

Address: _____

City: _____

State: _____ **Zip Code:** _____

Daytime Telephone: _____

Autographed copy to: _____

Autographed copy to: _____